WHO'S WHO IN INTERNATIONAL TENNIS

WHO'S WHO IN INTERNATIONAL TENNIS

EDITED BY DAVID EMERY

SPHERE BOOKS LIMITED
30–32 Gray's Inn Road, London WC1X 8JL

First published in Great Britain by
Sphere Books Ltd. 1983

Edited, designed and produced by First Editions (Rambletree Ltd.)

Set in Sabon by Inforum Ltd, Portsmouth

Printed and bound in Italy by
New Interlitho SpA.

Introduction

Few sports have enjoyed a boom such as the one tennis has been experiencing since the mid Seventies. The professional circuit, which began with just a handful of players, is now a year-long event, a travelling village which settles down for a week or a fortnight in cities throughout the world.

It is a glamorous world of mountainous prize money and massive media exposure. Where else, save perhaps Hollywood, would teenage girls be millionaires and household names?

Every year sees an influx of new, exciting talent competing for the rewards against the established stars like Borg, Connors, Chris Lloyd and Martina Navratilova.

The Who's Who in International Tennis is designed to capture that fluctuating world. It contains all the famous figures, plus an introduction to the would-be champions.

Several of the more veteran performers have also been included, even though they may be winding down their commitments on the tour, to give a complete reference book.

Sherry Acker

Born: June 16, 1959, Kalamazoo, Michigan, U.S.A.
Lives: Kalamazoo.
Height: 5–8. *Weight:* 140. Righthanded.
Career Highlights
U.S. Open: last 16 1979.
Avon Futures Championship: fourth place 1979; third place 1980.
USTA College Nationals: semi-finalist 1978.
U.S. Under 21 Championship: semi-finalist 1978.
Doubles
U.S. Open: semi-finalist 1979 (with Julie Anthony).
Avon Futures Championship: champion 1979 (with Mary Carillo).

Taught by her father, George, the coach at Kalamazoo College, Sherry turned pro in 1978 after attending the University of Florida. She was nominated for the Women's Tennis Association's Most Promising Newcomer Award in 1979. Enjoys writing and listening to music. Both her sisters, Judy and Gigi, are tennis players.

John Alexander

Born: July 4, 1951, Sydney, Australia.
Lives: Sydney and Atlanta, Georgia, U.S.A.
Height: 6–3. *Weight:* 175. Lefthanded.
Career Highlights
Australian Open: semi-finalist 1974, 1976, 1977.
WCT Finals: semi-finalist 1975; quarter-finalist 1973, 1979.
U.S. Clay Courts: semi-finalist 1981.
Led Australia to Davis Cup 1977.
Doubles
Wimbledon: finalist 1977 (with Dent), semi-finalist 1969 (with Dent).

John Alexander at Wimbledon 1978.

French Open: finalist 1975 (with Dent).
German Open: champion 1971 (with Gimeno).

'J.A.' as he's called became the youngest player ever to compete in a Davis Cup Challenge round when Harry Hopman pitched him into the match against the U.S. as a 17-year-old in 1968. He went on to lead Australia to their Cup win over Italy in 1977. A powerful server, he also performs surprisingly well on clay considering his upbringing. Disc trouble left him bedridden for four months in 1980, but his total recovery was proved when he won the Lambert and Butler Bristol tournament in 1982.

He reached No 8 in the world in 1975. Sister Sue is also a fine sportswoman. 'J.A.' enjoys yachting, surfing, golf and rugby.

Leslie Allen

Born: March 12, 1957, Cleveland, Ohio, U.S.A.
Lives: New York.
Height: 5–10. *Weight:* 145. Righthanded.
Career Highlights
U.S. Open: third round 1979.
French Open: third round 1979–80.
Toray Sillook (Tokyo): semi-finalist 1980.
Murjani-WTA Championships: quarter-finalist 1980.
Players Challenge (Montreal): quarter-finalist 1980.
Queensland Open: quarter-finalist 1977.
Australian Hard Courts: quarter-finalist 1977.
ATA National Championships: champion 1977.

The daughter of Broadway actress Sarah Allen, Leslie was sponsored for a time by American comedian Bill Cosby. A lively, articulate and intelligent girl, Leslie graduated with top honours in speech communication from the University of Southern California in 1977. She is also an expert on fashion and worked for a while as assistant to a New York designer. She is a natural athlete who was offered a track scholarship to Southern Methodist University in Dallas. She enjoys art and jazz in her spare time.

Leslie Allen.

Victor Amaya

Born: July 2, 1954, Denver, Colorado, U.S.A.
Lives: Goshen, Kentucky.
Height: 6–7. *Weight:* 225. Lefthanded.
Career Highlights
Wimbledon: last 32 1981.
U.S. Open: last 32 1979, 1980.
French Open: round of 32 1970, 1976.
Doubles
Wimbledon: quarter-finalist 1980 (with Pfister).
U.S. Open: quarter-finalist 1981 (with Pfister); finalist 1982.
French Open: champion 1980 (with Pfister).
WCT World: finalist 1981 (with Pfister).

'Big Vic', the amiable Alp of the circuit, has been seriously troubled by back trouble for the past couple of years. No joke when you stand 6ft 7in and are carrying around more than 16st. Born in Denver, he was raised in Puerto Rico and graduated from the University of

The Amritraj brothers, Vijay (left) and Anand.

Michigan with a degree in political science, having first studied medicine. He reads history and politics avidly and was elected on to the ATP Board of Directors in 1980.

On court, he is nimble for such a big man and possesses a thunderous, left-handed serve. He took Borg to five sets at Wimbledon in 1978 but lost there in 1982 to Britain's Buster Mottram. Married to Leslie with one daughter, Ashley.

Anand Amritraj

Born: March 20, 1952, Madras, India.
Lives: Marina del Ray, California, U.S.A.
Height: 6–1. *Weight:* 170. Righthanded.
Career Highlights
Queens: quarter-finalist 1980.
Costa Rica: quarter-finalist 1980.
Davis Cup: finalist 1974.
Indian Nationals: champion 1976.
Doubles
WCT World Championships: finalist 1982 (with brother Vijay).
Costa Rica: finalist 1980 (with Saviano).
Sao Paulo: champion 1980 (with Buehning).

Elder brother of Vijay and Ashok, Anand has failed to fulfil his early promise. He made his Davis Cup debut for India in 1968 and led them to the final in 1974, when they refused to play South Africa because of their apartheid policy. Fine doubles player. Married to Helen.

Vijay Amritraj

Born: December 14, 1953, Madras, India.
Lives: Madras and Los Angeles, U.S.A.
Height: 6–3. *Weight:* 160. Righthanded.
Career Highlights
Wimbledon: quarter-finalist 1973, 1981.
U.S. Open: quarter-finalist 1973, 1974.
WCT Finals: qualifier 1980, 1981.

WCT Challenge Cup: finalist 1981.
WCT Tournament of Champions: semi-finalist 1980.
Doubles
Wimbledon: quarter-finalist 1981 (with brother Anand).
WCT World: champion 1977 (with Stockton).
Davis Cup final 1974 (defaulted to South Africa over apartheid policy).

He has squired some of the world's most beautiful women, including Farrah Fawcett, but the glamorous, courteous Vijay, who plans a film career when he retires from tennis, is now engaged to marry 'by arrangement' an Indian girl, according to custom. Vijay, whose name means 'victory' in Hindi, burst onto the scene in 1973 at the age of 20, when he reached the quarter finals of Wimbledon and the U.S. Open. Wimbledon has been the stage for some of his most spectacular matches: in 1979 he led Borg two sets to one and 5–4 in the fourth set tie-break before losing; and in 1981 he was two sets to love up on Jimmy Connors in the quarter-final before Jimbo recovered to win in five.

The gentlemanly Vijay, with his wide toothpaste smile, has been an articulate ambassador for his sport and his country. He is a personal friend of Indian Prime Minister Indira Ghandi and many expect him eventually to turn to politics.

With brothers Anand and Ashok he owns Amritraj Productions, a film company in Hollywood. He has beaten all the top players, from Laver and Rosewall through to Borg and McEnroe. He led Los Angeles Strings to the 1978 World Team Tennis title and has been a member of India's Davis Cup side since 1968. Vijay refused to commit himself to the Volvo Grand Prix events in 1982 and had to qualify for Wimbledon. He is a graduate of Madras University in commerce and accountancy.

Matt Anger

Born: June 20, 1963, Walnut Creek, California, U.S.A.
Lives: Pleasamton, California.
Height: 6–1. *Weight:* 160. Righthanded.
Career Highlights
South African Juniors: champion 1981.
USTA Indoors: finalist 1980.
U.S. 18 & Under: semi-finalist 1980.

One of the world's top juniors in 1981, he is expected to have a fine future. A member of the U.S. Junior Davis Cup team.

Lea Antonoplis

Born: January 20, 1959, West Covina, California, U.S.A.
Lives: Glendora, California.
Height: 5–5. *Weight:* 145. Righthanded.
Career Highlights
Wimbledon Junior: champion 1977, quarter-finalist 1976.
Wimbledon Plate: quarter-finalist 1978, 1980.
U.S. Open Junior: finalist 1977.
Canadian Open: quarter-finalist 1979.
New South Wales Open: semi-finalist 1978.
U.S. Girls' 18's: semi-finalist 1975.
U.S. Girls' 18 Clay Courts: champion 1976; finalist 1975.
U.S. Girls' Hard Courts: finalist 1977.
U.S. Girls' 16's: champion 1975.
U.S. Girls' 16 Hard Courts: champion 1974.
Stockholm International Junior: champion 1977.

U.S. Amateur Indoor: semi-finalist 1977.
Maureen Conolly Cup team: 1976–77.
Doubles
Canadian Open: champion 1979 (with Jones).
U.S. Girls' 18: champion 1978 (with Kathy Jordan).

Despite a battle with the scales, Lea remains one of the most competitive players around. A graduate in business administration of the University of Southern California, she is a real outdoor girl, keen on water-skiing, sailing and golf. She also played saxophone in the school band.

Jimmy Arias

Born: August 16, 1964, Grand Island, New York, U.S.A.
Lives: Grand Island, New York.
Height: 5–6. *Weight:* 115. Righthanded.
Career Highlights
U.S. Open: second round 1980.
USTA/Penn: champion 1981.
Asawa: champion 1981.
Stowe: semi-finalist 1981.
South Orange: quarter-finalist 1981.
Doubles
French Open Mixed: champion 1981 (with Jaeger).

The youngest player to appear at the U.S. Open and to gain an ATP computer ranking, Jimmy has made a meteoric rise since turning pro in January 1981. Within 12 months he had rocketed into the top 100 and, with Andrea Jaeger, had captured the French Open Mixed Doubles championship. Brilliantly fast and slide-rule accurate, Jimmy confirmed his potential by beating Eliot Teltscher in the final of the USTA/Penn tournament at Shreveport in 1981.

Pablo Arraya.

Pablo Arraya

Born: October 21, 1961, Buenos Aires, Argentina.
Lives: Lima, Peru.
Height: 5–10. *Weight:* 160. Righthanded.
Career Highlights
State Express Classic: quarter-finalist 1982.
Turin: champion 1981.
Rio de Janiero: champion 1981.
Brasilia: champion 1981.
Madrid: finalist 1981.
Orange Bowl: finalist 1979.
South American Juniors: champion 1979.
Davis Cup for Peru.

The wisecracking Pablo introduced himself to the British public by humiliating national No 1 Buster Mottram in the State Express Classic at Bournemouth in 1982. Arraya, who had turned professional barely a year previously, triumphed in straight sets before falling to the eventual winner, Manuel Orantes in the following round.

John Austin

Born: July 31, 1957, Rolling Hills, California, U.S.A.
Lives: Torrance, California.
Height: 6–3. *Weight:* 175. Righthanded.
Career Highlights
Australian Open: last 16 1980.
Columbus Grand Prix: finalist 1981.
Las Vegas Grand Prix: quarter-finalist 1981.
Doubles
Wimbledon Mixed: champion 1980 (with sister Tracy).
NCAA: champion 1978 (with Nichols).

Brother of Tracy, John secured his own identity by climbing into the world's top 40 for a while in 1980. An All-American at UCLA, he is particularly effective on hard, fast surfaces. Easy-going John, a dependable rather than dynamic player, announced his arrival by beating McEnroe at Atlanta in 1980. That same year he teamed with Tracy to become the first brother–sister tandem to win the Wimbledon mixed doubles in the competition's 104-year history. He is married to LeAnne Harrison, a former touring professional, from Australia.

Tracy Austin

Born: December 12, 1962, Rolling Hills, California, U.S.A.
Lives: Rolling Hills.
Height: 5–4. *Weight:* 110. Righthanded.
Career Highlights
Wimbledon: semi-finalist 1979, 1980; last 16 1978.
U.S. Open: champion 1979, 1981; semi-finalist 1980; quarter-finalist 1978.
Italian Open: champion 1979.

John and Tracy Austin.

Avon Championships: champion 1980; finalist 1979.
Colgate Series Championships: finalist 1979.
Family Circle Cup: champion 1979, 1980; semi-finalist 1978.
Toyota Series: champion 1981.
U.S. Indoor: champion 1980; semi-finalist 1979.
Eastbourne: champion 1980, 1981.
Wimbledon Junior: champion 1978.
Wightman Cup team: 1978, 1979, 1981.
Federation Cup: 1978, 1979, 1980.
Doubles
Wimbledon Mixed: champion 1980 (with brother John).

Tracy has been a phenomenon from the moment she appeared on the tennis circuit with teeth braces and gingham dresses. She has never been ranked outside the top 25 from the first day she featured on the computer in July 1977 at the age of 14. She won the first event she ever entered on the pro tour – the Avon Futures of Portland, Oregon, in 1977. That same year she became the youngest to enter Wimbledon and the U.S. Open, and the youngest to be ranked inside the U.S. national top ten – she was No 4.

She entered the world top ten in March, 1978, after beating Martina Navratilova, to reach the finals of the Dallas tournament. Her record of 25 national titles obliterates the old mark of 17 held by Peaches Bartkowicz. She became the youngest player to represent the U.S.A. in either the Wightman Cup or Federation Cup, when she was selected for the squad in 1978.

She won her first major title in May 1979 when she ended Chris Lloyd's 125-match winning streak on clay in the semi-finals of the Italian Open and then beat Sylvia Hanika in the finals. And she became the youngest ever winner of the U.S. Open at 16 years and nine months in 1979. On her way to the title she beat: Madruga, Jaeger, Latham, Jordan, Hanika, Navratilova and Lloyd.

Tracy, whose mother Jeanne was ranked No 25 in Southern California and whose father is a nuclear physicist, had a disappointing season in 1982. Back trouble which had dogged her for months had just cleared, when a waiter poured boiling water over her arm and shoulders during a restaurant accident in California. She returned to reach the quarter-finals of Wimbledon, where she was beaten by Billie Jean King and the quarter-finals of both the French and U.S. Opens, where she fell each time to Hana Mandlikova. She is a member of a remarkable tennis family: elder sister Pam and brothers Jeff and John were national junior champions.

Tracy Austin.

Syd Ball

Born: January 24, 1950, Sydney, Australia.
Lives: Sydney.
Height: 6–2. *Weight:* 175. Righthanded.
Career Highlights
Surbiton: finalist 1974.
Hobart: quarter-finalist 1980.
Adelaide: semi-finalist 1981.
Brisbane: quarter-finalist 1981.

Once engaged to Britain's Sue Barker, Syd has earned a good, if unspectacular, living out of his tennis career. Though never a front runner, he has always been an honest performer who can be relied upon to justify his seeding. A fine doubles player, he has won eight Grand Prix events and been runner up in twelve others.

A typical Australian globetrotter, Ball has played in most countries but is now restricting his appearances.

Corrado Barazzutti

Born: February 19, 1953, Udine, Italy.
Lives: Rome.
Height: 5–10. *Weight:* 155.
Righthanded.
Career Highlights
U.S. Open: semi-finalist 1977.
French Open: semi-finalist 1978; junior champion 1971.
WCT Finals: semi-finalist 1978.
Grand Prix Masters: qualifier 1978.
Davis Cup team: champions 1976.

Nicknamed 'The Little Soldier' because of his straight-backed, military bearing, Corrado is one of the game's outstanding clay court performers. Son of a policeman, he was the hero of Italy's Davis Cup final triumph over Chile in Santiago in 1976 and has appeared in three other finals. His best year was 1978 when he reached the semi-finals of the French Open and U.S. Clay Courts. In the French Championship he was destroyed by Borg for the loss of only one game, but he has impressive career wins over the Swede as well as Jimmy Connors.

These achievements helped him move into the world's top ten for the year and he also qualified for the Masters and the WCT-Dallas Finals. He has slipped a little since then. He took up the sport at the age of nine and turned pro in 1972. Married to Barbara with a daughter, Giovanna.

Sue Barker

Born: April 19, 1956, Paignton, Devon, England.
Lives: Wimbledon.
Height: 5–5. *Weight:* 114.
Righthanded.
Career Highlights
Wimbledon: semi-finalist 1977, quarter-finalist 1976.
French Open: champion 1976.
Australian Open: semi-finalist 1975, 1978.
German Open: champion 1976.
Virginia Slims Championships: finalist 1977; fifth 1976.
Toyota Classic (Melbourne) – finalist 1976; semi-finalist 1977.
New South Wales Open: finalist 1975, 1977; semi-finalist 1979.
Swedish Open: champion 1974, 1975.
Wimbledon Plate: champion 1979.
Avon Championship: semi-finalist 1979.
Chichester: finalist 1979.
Wightman Cup: 1974–82.
Federation Cup: 1974–82.

Sue Barker.

Doubles
Wimbledon: semi-finalist 1978, 1981 (with Kiyomura).

Sue's form nosedived last year while her emotional life soared with her relationship with pop star Cliff Richard. The Devon blonde, coached by the uncompromising 'Mr (Arthur) Roberts', had her finest seasons in 1976 and 1977. She won the French Open title – admittedly at a time when many of the leading players were involved in Team Tennis – and then reached the semi-finals at Wimbledon. In a match she would have expected to win nine times out of ten, Sue went down to Dutchwoman Betty Stove and lost her chance of facing Virginia Wade in the Centenary Final. It was a blow from which she has never really recovered.

She reached No 4 in the world that year, but then began a gradual slump which was arrested by her stirring Daihatsu Challenge triumph of 1981, when she beat Tracy Austin en route to the title at Brighton. Sue became British No 1 in 1982, as age finally caught up with Virginia Wade. But she was sadly out of touch, losing in the first round of Wimbledon and choosing to miss the U.S. Open altogether.

Her devastating forehand is still one of the most powerful shots in the women's game. A born-again Christian – the religious philosophy brought her into touch with Cliff – Sue lives in Wimbledon, close to the All England Club.

Paolo Bertolucci

Born: August 3, 1954, Forte Dei Marmi, Italy.
Lives: Florence, Italy.
Height: 5–8. *Weight:* 170. Righthanded.
Career Highlights
Italian Open: semi-finalist 1973; quarter-finalist 1972.
German Open: champion 1977.
Florence: champion 1975, 1976.
Barcelona: champion 1976.
Hamburg: champion 1977.
Berlin: champion 1977.
Davis Cup: champions 1976.

The chunky 'Pasta Kid' plays where he chooses these days. But in his time he was one of the most feared opponents on European clay. He has competed in four Davis Cup finals and he and Adriano Panatta won the decisive doubles to clinch victory over Chile in 1976. He was beaten by Borg in Monte Carlo in 1982 in the Swede's comeback match.

Stanislov Birner

Born: October 11, 1956, Karlovy Vary, Czechoslovakia.
Lives: Pizen, Czechoslovakia.
Height: 5–7. *Weight:* 145. Righthanded.
Career Highlights
French Open: last 16 1978.
Washington Star: semi-finalist 1981.
Australian Satellite Circuit: champion 1979.
Doubles
Nice: finalist 1980 (with Hrebec).

'Stan' announced his arrival on the international scene by knocking Stan Smith out of the 1978 French Open. But it was the 1981 Washington Star Tournament which confirmed he was a star in the making. Then the Czech Davis Cup player with the double-fisted backhand beat Gene Mayer, Terry Moor and Mel Purcell before finding Jose Luis Clerc just a little too good. He is a fine doubles player. Single.

Renee Blount

Born: May 12, 1957, Washington D.C., U.S.A.
Lives: Carrollton, Texas.
Height: 5–4. *Weight:* 135. Righthanded.
Career Highlights
Toyota Classic (Melbourne): semi-finalist 1979.
Florida Federal Open (Tampa): quarter-finalist 1978.
Ellesse Grand Prix of Switzerland: finalist 1978.
Ellesse Grand Prix of Germany: semi-finalist 1978.
Providence, Rhode Island-WTA: quarter-finalist 1978.
Doubles
Stockholm Open: semi-finalist 1979 (with Hana Strachonova).

Renee, one of the exciting young black players to emerge in recent years, has one of the fastest serves in the women's game, officially timed at 100 mph. Nicknamed 'Pearl', she became the first black woman to win a pro tournament since Wimbledon champion Althea Gibson, when she took the 1979 Avon Futures of Columbus, Ohio. A surgeon's daughter, she turned pro in September 1978 and enjoys cooking and horseriding.

Nina Bohm

Born: April 30, 1958, Stockholm, Sweden.
Lives: Moindal, Sweden.
Height: 5–9. *Weight:* 130. Righthanded.
Career Highlights
Swedish Open: finalist 1980; semi-finalist 1979.
Wimbledon Junior: quarter-finalist 1976.
U.S. Open Junior: quarter-finalist 1976.
Queensland: champion 1975.
Swedish Junior Indoor: champion 1976.
Swedish Junior Clay Courts: champion 1976.
Stockholm Open: finalist 1977.
Annie Soisbault Cup team: 1976.
Brighton: quarter-finalist 1978.
Porsche Classic (Stuttgart): quarter-finalist 1978–79.
Federation Cup team: 1978–82.

A natural athlete, Nina won a local high jump competition at the age of 13 by clearing her own height of 4ft 11in. Started playing tennis at nine and was ranked fifth on the Swedish adult list in 1976, the same year she won the junior title. Daughter of a naval architect, she enjoys good literature and classical music.

Nina Bohm at Wimbledon.

Bjorn Borg.

Bjorn Borg

Born: June 6, 1956, Soldertaljie, near Stockholm, Sweden.
Lives: Monte Carlo, Monaco.
Height: 5–11. *Weight:* 162.
Righthanded.
Career Highlights
Wimbledon: champion 1976, 1977, 1978, 1979, 1980; finalist 1981.
U.S. Open: finalist 1976, 1978, 1980, 1981.
French Open: champion 1974, 1975, 1978, 1979, 1980, 1981.
WCT Finals: champion 1976; finalist 1974, 1975, 1979; semi-finalist 1978.
Masters: champion 1980, 1981; finalist 1978.
Italian Open: champion 1974, 1978.
Davis Cup: champions 1975.

Borg's march towards the pedestal as the world's greatest ever player was interrupted in 1982 by a squabble with the Men's Pro Council, when he refused to commit for the requisite number of Grand Prix events and was told he must therefore qualify for the major championships. Borg, who claimed he was a special case as he had always made it clear he wanted a four-month break from tennis, declined and took a year off.

Whether he will be the same implacable, virtually unbeatable force when he returns in 1983, no-one can be certain, although he showed few signs of ring rust when he beat McEnroe in his second come-back tournament in November 1982. But whatever happens Borg does not need to worry where the next meal is coming from. With the retirement of Muhammad Ali and the eye injury to Sugar Ray Leonard, he is comfortably the richest man in sport. Endorsements handled by Mark McCormack's agency bring him an income of more than £2 million a year. He owns a penthouse near his sports shop in Monte Carlo and a small island off the Swedish coast.

Borg's revolutionary double-handed backhand and ice-cool temperament have helped him to six French Open titles and a record five straight Wimbledon crowns. His defeat by McEnroe in the 1981 Wimbledon final was his first loss there in 42 matches. Despite all his success Borg still craves the U.S. Open title – '*only then can I call myself a great player*,' he says. He has reached the final four times, being beaten by Connors in 1976 and '78 and by McEnroe in '80 and '81. His Wimbledon defeat by McEnroe saw the Swede demoted from the world No 1 spot for the first time since 1978.

He started playing at the age of nine when his father, Rune, chose a tennis racket as a prize for winning a table tennis tournament and gave it to his son. By 15 he was playing Davis Cup for his country and at 18 he captured the French and Italian Open titles. In between he won the Wimbledon Junior crown, beating Buster Mottram in the final. At 19 he led Sweden to victory in the Davis Cup and a month after his 20th birthday he gained the first of his Wimbledon titles, beating Ilie Nastase in straight sets.

He married Romanian tennis professional Mariana Simionescu on July 24 1980 in one of the social events of the year, with a photographic company paying £100,000 for the rights to the ceremony and reception in Bucharest.

Borg warms up.

Mariana Borg (née Simionescu)

Born: November 21, 1956, Tirgu Neamt, Romania.
Lives: Monte Carlo, Monaco.
Height: 5–5. *Weight:* 120. Righthanded.
Career Highlights
Wimbledon: last 16 1977.
Japan Open: champion 1980.
Spanish Championships: finalist 1977.
Il Trofeo Gillette (Madrid): finalist 1977.
Tennis Week Open, South Orange, New Jersey: finalist 1975.
Monte Carlo: finalist 1977; quarter-finalist 1978, 1980.
Scottish Open: champion 1976.
French Open Junior: champion 1974.
U.S. Open Junior: quarter-finalist 1974, 1975.
Wimbledon Junior: finalist 1974.
Annie Soisbault Cup team: 1975.
Federation Cup team: 1973–75; 1978.
Doubles
Hahen Open: finalist 1976 (with Virginia Ruzici).

Married Bjorn Borg on July 24, 1980 and all but retired from international tennis. Mariana, who led Romania to the Federation Cup semi-final in 1973 with a victory over Britain's Joyce Hulme, reached No 38 in the world in 1978. She was seriously ill in 1982 with kidney stones.

Jeff Borowiak

Born: September 25, 1949, Lafayette, California, U.S.A.
Lives: Berkeley, California.
Height: 6–4. *Weight:* 180. Righthanded.

Mariana Borg with her husband.

Jeff Borowiak.

Career Highlights
Wimbledon: last 16 1971, 1981.
Canadian Open: champion 1977.
South African Open: finalist 1981.
U.S. National Junior: champion 1967.
NCAA Singles: champion 1970.
Doubles
NCAA: champion 1971.

One of the characters of the circuit, Borowiak endeared himself to Wimbledon crowds in 1981, by arriving for the tournament on a battered old bike which he parked by the dressing room wall while he played. The style obviously suited him for he reached the last 16, with victories over Brian Gottfried and Tim Gullikson, before falling to Peter McNamara.

A keen jogger, the long-legged Californian is also an accomplished musician, gaining a major at UCLA for the flute, piano and clarinet. He was U.S. National Junior Champion in 1967 and runner up in the prestigious, international junior event, the Orange Bowl in 1968. His best ranking was 25 in 1977. Married to Sheila with a son.

Lloyd Bourne

Born: October 18, 1958, Los Angeles, California, U.S.A.
Lives: Pasadena, California.
Height: 6–3. *Weight:* 180. Righthanded.
Career Highlights
Wimbledon: last 32 1982.
Hong Kong: quarter-finalist 1981.
Doubles
Bangkok: finalist 1981 (with Winitsky).

A Stanford University protegé, this black Californian came to prominence at Wimbledon '82, where he reached the third round, defeating Ilie Nastase on the way. But he met a sticky end when he played top seed John McEnroe, winning just four games. He first came on the computer at 555 in 1977, now he is approaching the top 50. Single.

Lloyd Bourne.

Iva Budarova

Born: July 31, 1960, Duchvoc, Czechoslovakia.
Lives: Prague, Czechoslovakia.
Height: 5–7¼. *Weight:* 145. Lefthanded.
Career Highlights
French Open Junior: quarter-finalist 1978.
Spanish Open: finalist 1979; quarter-finalist 1978.
Il Trofeo Gillette (Madrid): semi-finalist 1978.
Austrian Open: quarter-finalist 1979–80.
Turin, Italy: semi-finalist 1978.
Bonfiglio Cup Under 21 (Milan): finalist 1976.
Apple Bowl Junior: semi-finalist 1978.
Federation Cup: 1980–82.

Iva Budarova.

Iva is the forgotten girl of Czech tennis as Navratilova, Mandlikova and Marsikova have stormed the world. Coached by her father, Karel, her best shots are a powerful forehand and a cunning drop shot. Iva is interested in economics and wants to move into that field when she finishes with tennis. She had a disappointing 1982, losing in the first round at Wimbledon and the second at the French Open.

Fritz Buehning

Born: March 5, 1960, Summit, New Jersey, U.S.A.
Lives: Short Hills, New Jersey.
Height: 6–5. *Weight:* 195. Righthanded.
Career Highlights
New South Wales: champion 1980.
Johannesburg: finalist 1980.
American Junior Hard Courts: champion 1978.
Denver: semi-finalist 1981.
Atlanta: semi-finalist 1981.

Doubles
Sao Paulo: champion 1980 (with A. Amritraj).
Melbourne Indoor: champion 1980 (with Taygan).
Richmond, Virginia: champion 1980 (with Kreik).

Big Fritz's worst enemy is his explosive temper. Otherwise this 6ft 5in powerhouse has the strength and skill to go a long way.

Certainly he lacks nothing in background. His father was an Olympic gymnast for Germany and is now on the U.S. Olympic Committee, his elder brother was in the 1976 U.S. Olympic handball team, another brother was chosen for the Moscow Olympics team in 1980 and his sister, Susan, is a ranked tennis player in New Jersey. Buehning, whose hotel room is distinguishable by the noise of his cassette player, belonged to the same New Jersey club as Peter Fleming and followed him to UCLA, where he also played alongside

Eliot Teltscher and John Austin. He was an All American after two years at UCLA and turned pro just before the 1979 U.S. Open. By 1981 he was nudging the top 20 with victories over Guillermo Vilas and Jimmy Connors.

Bettina Bunge

Born: June 13, 1963, Adliswick, Switzerland.
Lives: Coral Gables, Florida, U.S.A.
Height: 5–7. *Weight:* 120. Righthanded.
Career Highlights
Wimbledon: semi-finalist 1982.
U.S. Open: third round 1978, 1980.
French Open: third round 1979, 1980.
New South Wales Open: finalist 1979.
African Eagle Classic: finalist 1979.
Italian Open: quarter-finalist 1980.
Eastbourne: quarter-finalist 1979.
Avon Championships of Kansas City: quarter-finalist 1980.
Avon Championships of Dallas: quarter-finalist 1980.
Chichester: quarter-finalist 1980.
U.S. Girls' 16 Hard Courts: champion 1978.
U.S. Girls' 16 Clay Courts: finalist 1978.
Orange Bowl: semi-finalist 1978.
Federation Cup: 1980.

A walking United Nations of women's tennis, the attractive, blond Bettina was born in Switzerland, raised in Peru, lives in America and considers herself a

Bettina Bunge.

German citizen, like her father Siegfried, a dealer in fish food. Bettina, who speaks German, Spanish and French as well as English, was national champion of Peru before being ranked No 2 on the U.S. Girls' age 16 list for 1978, behind Tracy Austin. She leapt to world No 22 in 1980 and confirmed her progress in 1982 by reaching the Wimbledon semi-final.

'I'm gaining in confidence all the time,' she warned. *'I know I'm capable of winning a big tournament.'*

Mike Cahill

Born: June 17, 1952, Waukesha, Wisconsin, U.S.A.
Lives: Memphis, Tennessee.
Height: 6–0. *Weight:* 165. Righthanded.
Career Highlights
U.S. Open: last 16 1981.
Stowe: finalist 1979.
Doubles
Stowe: champion 1979 (with Krulevitz).
Tokyo/Seiko: finalist 1979 (with Moor).
Tel Aviv: finalist 1979 (with Dibley).
Bangkok: champion 1981 (with Austin).
Memphis: finalist 1981 (with Tom Gullikson).

Mike, who holds a degree in history and religion from Alabama, pushed his name to the forefront in the 1981 U.S. Open when he beat Johan Kriek en route to the fourth round. He had missed several months of the previous season because of the illness of his wife Jamie. He confirmed his comeback by teaming with Tom Gullikson to shock McEnroe and Fleming on the way to the final of the U.S. National Indoor doubles at Memphis. He has a daughter.

Ricardo Cano

Born: February 26, 1951, Buenos Aires, Argentina.
Lives: Buenos Aires.
Height: 5–7. *Weight:* 150. Righthanded.
Career Highlights
Cuneo: champion 1980.
Campinas: champion 1980.
ATP/Buenos Aires: semi-finalist 1980.
South Orange: quarter-finalist 1980.
Cairo: semi-finalist 1981.
Nice: quarter-finalist 1981.
Monte Carlo: quarter-finalist 1981.
Tokyo: quarter-finalist 1981.
Indianapolis: quarter-finalist 1981.
Boston: quarter-finalist 1981.
Doubles
Bournemouth: champion 1981 (with Pecci).
Brussels: champion 1981 (with Gomez).

Cano won recognition throughout South America in 1977 when he inspired Argentina's upset of the United States in the Davis Cup by beating Dick Stockton. But it wasn't until he had turned 30 in 1981 that the staunch family man made his real breakthrough in world terms. The clay court specialist had previously preferred to play the South American circuit so as to be close to his wife Claudia and their two daughters, Dolores and Victoria. His move to the main tour paid immediate dividends as he reached the semi-final in Cairo and six other quarter-finals.

David Carter

Born: April 21, 1956, Budaberg, Australia.
Lives: Budaberg.
Height: 6–0. *Weight:* 165. Righthanded.
Career Highlights

Mexico City: finalist 1981.
Quito: finalist 1981.
Sarasota: semi-finalist 1980.
South Orange: semi-finalist 1980.
Doubles
Vina del Mar: champion 1981 (with Kronk)
Mar del Plata: champion 1981 (with Kronk).
Munich: champion 1981 (with Kronk); finalist 1980 (with Lewis).
Kitzbuhel: champion 1981 (with Kronk).

He reached the last 32 of Wimbledon in 1982 before losing to Nick Saviano. The bearded Carter, who plays the typical Australian game of serve and volley, joined the tour in 1975 and has improved steadily ever since, until breaking into the top 100 in 1981. Married to Karen.

Rosemary Casals

Born: September 16, 1948, San Francisco, California.
Lives: Sausalito, California, U.S.A.
Height: 5–2½. *Weight:* 116. Righthanded.
Career Highlights
Wimbledon: semi-finalist 1967, 1969, 1970, 1972.
U.S. Open: finalist 1970, 1971; semi-finalist 1966, 1969.
Family Circle Cup: champion 1973; semi-finalist 1974.
Virginia Slims Circuit: eight titles 1970–78.
Wightman Cup team: 1967, 1976–81.
Federation Cup team: 1976–81.
Doubles
Wimbledon: champion 1967–68, 1970–71, 1973 (with King); finalist 1980 (with Turnbull).
U.S. Open: champion 1967, 1971, 1974, (with King); finalist 1968–69, 1973, 1975, (with King); champion, 1982 (with Turnbull); finalist 1981 (with Turnbull).
French Open: finalist 1968, 1970 (with King).

Rosie Casals.

Half of the best known doubles act in women's tennis during the late Sixties and early Seventies, Rosie was more than just Billie Jean King's partner. She was ranked world No 5 at singles in 1976 and twice reached the final of the U.S. Open, where she lost to Margaret Court in 1970 and Mrs King in 1971. Player-coach to the U.S. Wightman Cup team in 1977, '79 and '80, she was also Federation Cup captain in 1980. Rosie, daughter of an El Salvador soccer player, is a keen drummer – but an even keener politician in the women's tennis movement. She heads Women in Tennis, an organisation which helps arrange sponsorship deals, and serves on the WTA Board of Directors.

Ross Case

Born: November 1, 1951, Toowoomba, Australia.
Lives: Newport Beach, California.
Height: 5–8. *Weight:* 155. Righthanded.
Career Highlights
Australian Open: quarter-finalist 1977.
Las Vegas: finalist 1975.
Doubles
Wimbledon: champion 1977; finalist 1976 (with Masters).
French Open: finalist 1979 (with Dent).
Australian Open: champion 1977, finalist 1976 (with Masters).
Mexico City: finalist 1981 (with Alexander).
Cleveland: finalist 1981 (with Ball).

So lightning fast around court that he is nicknamed the 'Snake', Case has been reduced to more human levels recently by a shoulder injury. He plays an all-out attacking game which makes him one of the most entertaining players. His greatest success in singles came in 1975 when he was beaten in the final of the Alan King Classic in Las Vegas by Roscoe Tanner. King was so impressed by his performance that he upped Ross's prize money to equal Tanner's. Case's reflexes have made him one of the finest of modern day doubles players, winning Wimbledon and the French and Australian Opens.

Evonne Cawley (née Goolagong)

Born: July 21, 1951, Griffith, New South Wales, Australia.
Lives: Hilton Head Island, South Carolina, U.S.A.
Height: 5–6. *Weight:* 127. Righthanded.
Career Highlights
Wimbledon: champion 1971, 1980; finalist 1972, 1975, 1976; semi-finalist 1973, 1978, 1979.

Evonne Cawley with the Wimbledon Singles Trophy.

U.S. Open: finalist 1973–1976; quarter-finalist 1979.
Australian Open: champion 1974, 1975, 1976, 1978; finalist 1971, 1973.
French Open: champion 1971; finalist 1972; semi-finalist 1973.
Italian Open: champion 1973; semi-finalist 1979.
South African Open: champion 1972; finalist 1971, 1973.
Canadian Open: champion 1972, 1973; finalist 1971.
U.S. Indoor: champion 1973, 1979; finalist 1975.
U.S. Clay Courts: finalist 1972, 1979; semi-finalist 1980.
Virginia Slims Championships: champion 1974, 1976; finalist 1973, 1978.

Virginia Slims Circuit events: 10 titles; 1974–76, 1978.
Avon Championships: third place, 1980.
Colgate Series Championships: sixth place, 1979.
Chichester: champion 1978, 1979; finalist 1980.
Federation Cup Team: 1971–76.
Doubles
Wimbledon: champion 1974 (with Michel); finalist 1971 (with Court).
Wimbledon Mixed: finalist 1972 (with Warwick).
Australian Open: champion 1974, 1975 (with Michel).
Italian Open: finalist 1979 (with Reid).
French Open Mixed: champion 1972 (with Warwick).

Wimbledon's favourite mum is now over 30 and attempting her second comeback from motherhood. But she remains one of the most graceful and best loved players of all time. Born in Griffith, New South Wales, she was brought up in nearby Barellan, a town of 900 souls, the third of eight children to Ken and Melinda Goolagong. Part aborigine, Evonne showed a natural aptitude for all sports, playing rugby, cricket and soccer as a child before developing her tennis talent. She was spotted by coach Vic Edwards and taken into his Sydney home.

She entered the international scene in 1970 and a year later had captivated everyone by winning Wimbledon and celebrating with a shopping spree down the King's Road. It was nine years before she was to win the All England crown again and by then she had married English businessman Roger Cawley, a former Sussex player, and given birth to daughter, Kelly Inala, in 1977. She has won every major title going except the U.S. Open – where she has four times lost in the final – and in 1979 became the fifth woman to win one million dollars in tournament play, joining Billie Jean King, Chris Lloyd, Martina Navratilova and Virginia Wade. The Cawleys have invested some of their money into 70 acres on Hilton Head Island, South Carolina, and plan to build a tennis ranch there when Evonne retires. In 1981 she gave birth to their son, Morgan, and attempted to return the following season, with moderate success.

José-Luis Clerc

Born: August 16, 1958. Buenos Aires, Argentina.
Lives: Buenos Aires.
Height: 6–1. *Weight:* 175. Righthanded.
Career Highlights
Wimbledon: last 32 1981.

José-Luis Clerc.

U.S. Open: last 16 1981.
Italian Open: champion 1981.
French Open: semi-finalist 1981.
U.S. Clay Courts: champion 1980, 1981.
U.S. Pro: champion 1981.
South American Open: champion 1978, 1980.
U.S. Open Junior: finalist 1976.
French Open Junior: finalist 1976.

Clerc counts himself lucky to be walking, let alone playing tennis. After a horrific fall through a hotel's glass roof in Dinard, France, in 1975, he needed almost 50 stitches and a surgeon's skill to repair his left thigh. He spent eight months convalescing before returning to rocket up the rankings. His best year was 1981 when he captured the Italian Open, beating Lendl on the way, and reached the semi-final of the French Open with a victory over Connors. He followed that by reeling off four consecutive Super Series victories, a run of 24 wins in 28 days to move to world No 5 overtaking Vilas as Argentinian No 1.

With two such world class players to call on, Argentina have found great success recently in the Davis Cup. Clerc beat McEnroe in the quarter-finals in 1980 to help Argentina into the semi-finals where they lost to Lendl-inspired Czechoslovakia. In 1981 he helped destroy Britain in the semi-final when Argentina reached the final before falling to the U.S.A.

Coached by Pat Rodriguez, his former mentor with the national junior team, Clerc is primarily a clay court specialist. But his all-round game is improving gradually. He reached the last 32 at Wimbledon in 1981 and the last 16 of the U.S. Open. He boycotted Wimbledon in 1982 because of the Falklands conflict. Clerc is married to Annalie, with a son, Juan Pablo.

Glynis Coles

Born: February 20, 1954, London, England.
Lives: London.
Height: Height: 5–8. *Weight:* 136. Righthanded.
Career Highlights
Wimbledon: last 16 1975.
Swedish Open: champion 1973; semi-finalist 1977.
Spanish Championships: finalist 1974.
Paris Indoor: semi-finalist 1975.
Swiss Open: champion 1975.
Indiana WTA: champion 1978.
Dewar Cup (London): semi-finalist 1973.
Eastbourne: quarter-finalist 1975.
Wimbledon Junior: finalist 1972.
Wightman Cup team: 1973–76, 1980, 1981.
Federation Cup team: 1974–75, 1980.

Glynis, the youngest player ever to win the British under 21 championship – beating Veronica Burton in 1971 when she was 17 – is the great niece of Mildred Coles, who played in the 1908 Olympics in London. A fine squash player and a keen chess enthusiast, Glynis reached No 39 in the world in 1975, when she beat Rosie Casals to reach the semis of the Paris Indoor and Martina Navratilova to reach the quarters at Eastbourne. Four times ranked third in Britain, she was a member of the Wightman Cup team in 1973–76 and 1980–81 and the Federation Cup team in 1974–75 and 1980. She was educated at Chiswick Poly and is a fine doubles player.

Jimmy Connors

Born: September 2, 1952, Belleville, Illinois, U.S.A.
Lives: Miami Beach, Florida.
Height: 5–10. *Weight:* 155.

Lefthanded.

Career Highlights

Wimbledon: champion 1974, 1982; finalist 1975, 1977, 1978; semi-finalist: 1979, 1980, 1981.

U.S. Open: champion: 1974, 1976, 1978, 1982; finalist 1975, 1977; semi-finalist: 1979, 1980, 1981.

French Open: semi-finalist 1979, 1980; quarter-finalist 1981.

Australian Open: champion 1974; finalist 1975.

Grand Prix Masters: champion 1977; semi-finalist 1972, 1973, 1979, 1980.

WCT Finals: champion 1977, 1980; semi-finalist 1979.

U.S. Clay Courts: champion 1974, 1976, 1978, 1979; finalist 1972, 1977.

U.S. Pro Indoor: champion 1976, 1978, 1979.

U.S. Indoor: champion 1973, 1974, 1975, 1978, 1979.

South African Open: champion 1973, 1974.

Doubles (with Nastase)

Wimbledon: champion 1973.

U.S. Open: champion 1975.

French Open: finalist 1973.

U.S. Open mixed: finalist 1974 (with Evert).

The greatest fighter in the game returned in triumph in 1982 to claim his fourth U.S. Open title and his second Wimbledon crown after a gap of eight years. In that time Jimbo, the brash Belleville Basher whose mom, Gloria, used to scream encouragement from the stands, has matured into a more even-tempered family man with wife Patti, a former Playboy pin-up, and son Brett. At 30 he believes his best years could be ahead of him, remarkable for a man who dominated the Seventies along with Borg.

Jimmy Connors.

The people's champion – Jimmy Connors.

Connors attended the University of California at Los Angeles where he was an All American and National Intercollegiate Champion in 1971. His mother, Gloria, a teaching professional, was a touring player and ranked 13th among national juniors and No 2 in Missouri. Connors and his double-fisted backhand really burst through in 1974, when he destroyed Rosewall to win Wimbledon and then followed up with the U.S. and Australian crowns.

In that year he lost only four matches and set a record for win percentages in the Open era of .960. It made him indisputably No 1 in the world, but the following year he suffered defeat in the same three finals, losing to veterans Ashe (Wimbledon), Orantes (U.S.) and Newcombe (Australia). The next year a young fair-haired Swede captured his first Wimbledon title and although Connors remained No 1 on the computer until 1978, it was a point of statistics rather than fact. With Borg dropping out of circulation last year, Connors seemed to shake off the mental barrier.

He gave notice that he was gunning for the top again when he beat McEnroe, then the current No 1, in a rowdy Benson and Hedges final at Wembley.

He followed that by again mastering the New Yorker at Queens before confirming his superiority with an epic Wimbledon triumph 3–6 6–3 6–7 7–6 6–4. And to prove his metamorphosis from public enemy No 1 to people's champion was complete, he even said a courteous 'thank you' when Wimbledon presented him with the Commemorative Medal he had declined to accept in 1977.

Two months later Connors was at his favourite battle ground in New York to destroy Lendl in the final of the U.S. Open. *'I'm content with my life now,'* he said. Well he might be.

Mark Cox

Born: July 5, 1943, Leicester, England.
Lives: Ashtead, Surrey.
Height: 6–1. *Weight:* 170.
Righthanded.
Career Highlights
Wimbledon: last 16 1979.
U.S. Open: quarter-finalist 1966.
Australian Open: quarter-finalist 1967, 1971.
WCT Finals: qualifier 1975.
South African Open: quarter-finalist 1973.
Stockholm Open: champion 1976.
Stuttgart: finalist 1980.
British Hard Courts: champion 1970; semi-finalist 1971.
Dewar Cup: champion 1969.
Doubles
Wimbledon: semi-finalist 1966

An economics graduate from Cambridge University, Mark made history when he became the first amateur to defeat a professional at the dawning of Open tennis in 1968 . . . he beat Pancho Gonzales in the British Hard Courts Championships. One of the original players on the first regular WCT tour in 1971, he has always been a solid performer. In recent years his best results have been in Davis Cup for Great Britain, particularly in doubles with David Lloyd. He was instrumental in Britain reaching the Davis Cup final against the U.S. in 1978. He and Lloyd were the surprise packet of the 1979 Braniff Airways World Doubles Championship when they reached the semi-finals before losing to the eventual winners, Peter Fleming and John McEnroe. Cox is a commentator on tennis for the BBC. He is married to Allison, with sons Julian and Steven and daughter Lorraine.

Kevin Curren

Born: March 2, 1958, Durban, South Africa.
Lives: Durban and Austin, Texas, U.S.A.
Height: 6–1. *Weight:* 170. Righthanded.
Career Highlights
Wimbledon: last 16, 1980.
U.S. Open: last 16, 1981.
Johannesburg Grand Prix: champion 1981.
Doubles
Wimbledon: quarter-finalist 1980; semi-finalist 1982 (with Denton); mixed champion 1982 (with Smith).
U.S. Open: quarter-finalist 1981 (with Denton); round of 16 1980 (with Denton); champion 1982; mixed champion 1982 (with Smith).
U.S. Clay Courts: champion 1980, 1981 (with Denton).
WCT World: finalist 1982 (with Denton).

The former South African junior champion was encouraged by countryman Cliff Drysdale to export his talent to America. He did – to the University of Texas – becoming an All American in 1979, the same year he captured the NCAA singles title. It was at University that Curren met Steve Denton and formed the highly successful doubles partnership that carried them to the Wimbledon quarter-final in 1980 and the semi-final in 1982 where they lost to Fleming and McEnroe.

The athletic Curren, who also enjoys soccer, cricket, rugby and squash, believes he must conquer his own fierce will to win if he is to fulfil his potential. *'I want to do well so badly I get myself uptight thinking about computer*

Kevin Curren.

points,' he says. '*I know I've just got to relax and play my natural game.*' He did just that at Beckenham in 1982 when he defeated Buster Mottram in the final.

José-Luis Damiani

Born: November 21, 1956, Montevideo, Uruguay.
Lives: Montevideo.
Height: 6–1. *Weight:* 180. Righthanded.
Career Highlights
Gstaad: quarter-finalist 1981.
Boston: quarter-finalist 1981.
Indianapolis: quarter-finalist 1981.
Geneva: quarter-finalist 1981.
Doubles
Palermo: champion 1981 (with Perez).

This quiet, studious man who completed two years of medical school before turning his hand to pro tennis, has been the Uruguay No 1 since 1976. A bearded, powerful figure, he turned pro in 1977 and broke into the world's top 100 after success on the Italian satellite circuit, where he won four out of five tournaments. He quarreled with officialdom during the 1982 Bournemouth tournament and stormed home vowing never to play in Britain again. Married to Adriana with a son, Alejandro.

Martin Davis

Born: November 15, 1958, San José, California, U.S.A.
Lives: San José.
Height: 6–0. *Weight:* 175. Righthanded.
Career Highlights
Hong Kong: semi-finalist 1981.
Doubles
Mexico City: champion 1981 (with Dunk).
Hong Kong: finalist 1981 (with Drewett).

A Californian who is improving at a steady pace, Davis worked his way out of the 400's to the verge of the top 100 with some consistent but unspectacular victories. He lost in straight sets to John McEnroe in the second round of the U.S. Open in 1982 but showed he is no slouch, taking 13 games off the defending champion. Single.

Phil Dent

Born: February 14, 1950, Sydney, Australia.
Lives: Sydney and Newport Beach, California, U.S.A.
Height: 6–0. *Weight:* 175. Righthanded.
Career Highlights
Wimbledon: quarter-finalist 1977; last 16, 1980.
French Open: semi-finalist 1977; junior champion 1968.
Italian Open: semi-finalist 1977.
Australian Open: quarter-finalist 1968; junior champion 1968.
Davis Cup: champions 1977.
Doubles
Wimbledon: semi-finalist 1971 (with Alexander).
U.S. Open Mixed: champion 1976 (with King).
French Open: finalist 1977 (with Alexander).
Australian Open: champion 1975 (with Alexander); finalist 1970, 1973, 1977 (with Alexander).

A keen student of The Turf, the likeable 'Philby' owns several racehorses in partnership with other touring pros. But it's his thoroughbred serve and volley game, plus his doubles prowess,

Phil Dent.

which has thrilled the world's tennis watchers. He took up the game at eight and, under the wing of the legendary Harry Hopman, made his debut for Australia's Davis Cup team at 17 along with his doubles partner, John Alexander.

He had his best year in 1977 when he reached the semi-final of both the French and Italian Opens, the quarter finals of Wimbledon and climbed to No 22 in the world. Since then his success has mainly come with others – in doubles with Alexander, mixed doubles with Billie Jean King and team events with Australia. He was a member of the Aussie squad which won the Nations Cup in 1979 and was in the 1981Davis Cup team which reached the semi-finals before losing to the U.S. Polite and approachable, golf-enthusiast Dent married former women tennis star Betty Anne Stuart and they had their first child, a son called Taylor, in May 1981.

Steve Denton

Born: September 5, 1956, Kingsville, Texas.
Lives: Austin, Texas.
Height: 6–2. *Weight:* 180. Righthanded.
Career Highlights
U.S. Open: fourth round 1982.
South African Open: semi-finalist 1981.
Canadian Open: quarter-finalist 1981.
Doubles
Wimbledon: quarter-finalist 1980 (with Curren).
U.S. Open: champion 1982; quarter-finalist 1981; last 16 1980 (with Curren)
U.S. Clay Courts: champion 1980, 1981 (with Curren).

In the space of four spectacular months in 1981, 'The Bull' as Denton is known, climbed from 440 in the world to 24 with his power-packed game. He went on to prove it no fluke at the U.S. Open in 1982, where he and Kevin Curren took the doubles title. An asthma sufferer as a child, he was advised to keep away from games on grass and switched from baseball and football to tennis. He teamed up with Curren at the University of Texas and one of the world's best doubles partnerships was born. He also met coach Warren Jacques, an Australian player from the Laver-Rosewall era who helped develop his game.

The main block to his progress was

his massive size, but with strict dieting Steve lost 25 pounds – and began to pick up fat pay-packets. He still remains a powerful figure, as John McEnroe knows: the New Yorker offended Denton during the 1982 Wimbledon and the tall Texan threatened to thump him in the dressing room. Single.

Diane Desfor

Born: June 15, 1955, Long Beach, California, U.S.A.
Lives: Los Angeles.
Height: 5–5. *Weight:* 125. Righthanded.
Career Highlights
Canadian Open: semi-finalist 1978, 1979.
NSW Classic: semi-finalist 1979.
Eastbourne: quarter-finalist 1980.
World Tennis Classic (Montreal): quarter-finalist 1979.
Chichester: quarter-finalist 1978.
Wells Fargo Open (San Diego): quarter-finalist 1980.
South Australian Open: quarter-finalist 1979.
Doubles (with Hallquist)
U.S. Open: quarter-finals 1979, 1980.
Beckenham: champion 1980.
N.S.W. Open: champion 1979.

The blonde from Long Beach graduated from the University of Southern California as a Phi Beta Kappa with a degree in psychology and was such a fine student she has been awarded a graduate scholarship and will return when her tennis career ends. She has served as vice president of the Women's Tennis Association and head of the Ranking Committee and is a past winner of the Player Service Award. A fine doubles player, mainly with Barbara Hallquist.

Eddie Dibbs

Born: February 23, 1951, Brooklyn, New York, U.S.A.
Lives: Miami, Florida.
Height: 5–7. *Weight:* 160. Righthanded.
Career Highlights
U.S. Open: quarter-finalist 1979.
French Open: semi-finalist 1975, 1976; quarter-finalist 1979.
Italian Open: semi-finalist 1976, 1978, 1979.
German Open: champion 1973, 1974, 1976.
WCT Finals: finalist 1978; semi-finalist 1977.
WCT Tournament of Champions: champion 1981; finalist 1982.

'Fast' Eddie is running out of a bit of steam these days, but he was still good enough to beat McEnroe in the semi-final of the WCT Tournament of Champions at Forest Hills in 1982, before losing to Lendl. A baseball star at school, Eddie also tried pro football but was too small. His switch to tennis paid handsome dividends. He had his best year in 1978 when he finished third in the Grand Prix points table, but claimed the £150,000 first prize when the two top finishers, Connors and Borg failed to play the required number of tournaments. His total prize money for the season was £250,000. Single.

Colin Dibley

Born: September 19, 1944, Marrickville, Australia.
Lives: Chatham, New Jersey, U.S.A.
Height: 6–2. *Weight:* 180. Righthanded.
Career Highlights
Wimbledon: quarter-finalist 1971, 1972; last 16 1980.
Australian Open: semi-finalist 1979;

quarter-finalist 1974.
Australian Hard Courts: champion 1970.
U.S. Open 35's: champion 1980.
Davis Cup: 1971–74.
Doubles
Adelaide: champion 1981 (with James).
Metz: champion 1980 (with G. Mayer).

Now reaching the venerated stage of veteran, 'Dibbs' has been one of the most respected players on the circuit, especially on grass. Twice a Wimbledon quarter-finalist, his strong serve and volley game troubled the best. He had his finest year in 1977 when he was ranked 36 in the world. A former customs officer at Sydney Airport before trying out the circuit, he is married to Carol, with a son, Shea.

Colin Dibley.

Brad Drewett

Born: July 19, 1958, Killarney Heights, Australia.
Lives: Killarney Heights.
Height: 6–0. *Weight:* 175. Lefthanded.
Career Highlights
Wimbledon: last 16 1979.
New South Wales: quarter-finalist 1979.
Adelaide: finalist 1981.
South Orange: quarter-finalist 1981.
Doubles
Newport: champion 1981 (with Van Dillen).
Linz: finalist 1981 (with Slozil).
Hong Kong: finalist 1981 (with M. Davis).

A hit and miss player – popular with the ladies (he's blond and single!). His record from his junior days is attractive, but since then? A couple of quarter-finals and a runners-up spot in Adelaide is all he has to show so far, although with his talent his day must surely come. He was Australian junior champion in 1975, a semi-finalist in 1976 and reached the Wimbledon Junior semis in 1975 and '76.

Pat DuPré

Born: September 16, 1954, Liège, Belgium.
Lives: La Jolla, California, U.S.A.
Height: 6–3. *Weight:* 175. Righthanded.
Career Highlights
Wimbledon: semi-finalist 1979.
U.S. Open: quarter-finalist 1979, last 32 1981.
ATP Championship: semi-finalist 1980.

When Pat bent over to pick up an LP record album at his home in 1979 he almost ended his tennis career. He slipped a disc and spent months convalescing. At that stage he was ranked 18 in the world having reached the Wimbledon semi-finals and the U.S. quarters. He struggled to regain his touch until teaming up with Dennis Ralston as his coach.

Born in Liège of Belgian parents, Pat emigrated to America at the age of three. An outstanding junior, he was an All American at Stanford University, won the U.S. 18 age group singles title and shared No 1 junior ranking with Gerulaitis in 1972. A fine sportsman who always carries himself with dignity, Pat has received the American Youth Award, given to American athletes who have exerted the greatest influence for good on American youth. He is married to Darcy.

Jo Durie

Born: July 27, 1960, Bristol, England.
Lives: Bristol.
Height: 5–11½. *Weight:* 140. Righthanded.
Career Highlights
Wimbledon: last 16 1981.
Wimbledon Plate: semi-finalist 1979.

Pat DuPré.

Wimbledon Junior: semi-finalist 1978.
German Indoor Open: semi-finalist 1978.
Beckenham: finalist 1980, semi-finalist 1977.
Trophee Pernod Lee on Solent: champion 1979.
Cumberland: champion 1979, 1980, 1981.
Goteborg, Sweden: champion 1978.
Orange Bowl: semi-finalist 1978.
British Junior Grass Courts: champion 1977.
Wightman Cup team: 1979, 1981, 1982.

Doubles

British Hard Courts: champion 1978 (with Jevans).
Beckenham: champion 1979 (with Jevans).

The Bristol bank manager's daughter was almost forced to quit tennis because of severe back problems. But an intricate operation in 1980, which could have left her crippled, righted the injury and she has gone on to the greatest success of her career. In 1982 the tall former Clifton High pupil was the best ranked British women on the world computer, but Jo's thrilling three-set defeat by Virginia Wade at Wimbledon – after she had beaten Sue Barker in Edgbaston – just prevented her from outright claim to the title of national No 1.

The previous year she had reached the last 16 at Wimbledon to confirm the promise shown back in 1978 when she was No 1 British junior. She took part in Britain's lone success during the 1982 Wightman Cup, teaming with Anne Hobbs to beat Rosie Casals and Anne Smith. Coached by Alan Jones, she enjoys music, reading and films, and supports Bristol City.

Jo Durie.

Klaus Eberhard

Born: September 15, 1957, Dattelm, West Germany.
Lives: Hanover.
Height: 5–5. *Weight:* 155. Righthanded.
Career Highlights
Berlin: quarter-finalist 1979.
Kitzbuhel: semi-finalist 1981.
Tel Aviv: semi-finalist 1981.
Mexico City: quarter-finalist 1981.
Doubles
Kitzbuhel: champion 1980 (with Marten).
Nancy: champion 1979 (with Meiler).

A consistent player who occasionally pulls off the odd surprise like beating Victor Pecci to reach the semi finals at Kitzbuhel in 1981. His best showing on the world computer was 104 in 1980. Single.

Mark Edmondson.

Mark Edmondson

Born: June 28, 1954, Gosford, Australia.
Lives: Sydney, Australia.
Height: 6–1. *Weight:* 190. Righthanded.
Career Highlights
Wimbledon: semi-finalist 1982.
Australian Open: champion 1976, semi-finalist 1981.
Davis Cup: champions 1977.
Doubles
Australian Open: champion 1980, 1981 (with Warwick).
Italian Open: champion 1980 (with Warwick).

The shock winner of the 1976 Australian Open when he beat Rosewall and Newcombe in successive matches, the powerful 'Edo' proved he was no one-day wonder when he bludgeoned his way through to the Wimbledon semi-final in 1982, before losing to Connors. Tough talking and occasionally truculent, he has been a regular in the Australian Davis Cup team since 1976 and has served on the board of directors of the Association of Tennis Professionals. His switchback career hit a peak in 1981 when he gate-crashed the top 20 for the first time. A fine doubles player he collected the Italian and Australian Open titles with Kim Warwick. Married to Vicki.

Peter Elter

Born: June 10, 1958, Essen, West Germany.
Lives: Essen.
Height: 5–10. *Weight:* 170. Righthanded.
Career Highlights
Indian Open: finalist 1979.

Wimbledon Junior: finalist 1976.
Cairo: finalist 1981.
Stockholm: quarter-finalist 1981.

An allergy brought on by pollen slowed down Peter's initial progress. Twice German national champion, he tore ligaments in both feet in 1981 and needed surgery. A hand injury and then the pollen aversion dogged him and he was out for several months. His father was a top class soccer player.

Chris Evert Lloyd *see* Chris Lloyd

Chris Evert married John Lloyd in 1979.

Rosalyn Fairbank.

Rosalyn Fairbank

Born: November 2, 1960, Durban, South Africa.
Lives: Durban.
Height: 5–8. *Weight:* 140. Righthanded.
Career Highlights
Wimbledon Plate: champion 1980.
New South Wales Building Society Classic: finalist 1979.
New South Wales Open: quarter-finalist 1979.
South African Open: quarter-finalist 1978.

Trophee Pernod West Worthing: finalist 1979.
Trophee Pernod Lee on Solent: finalist 1979; semi-finalist 1980.
Wells Fargo Tennis Open: quarter-finalist 1980.
Orange Bowl Junior International: finalist 1979.
Pepsi Junior Masters: finalist 1979.
Eastbourne Under 21: semi-finalist 1978.
Beckenham Under 21: semi-finalist 1978.

This schoolgirl swimming champion made her tennis breakthrough in 1979 in junior competitions. She reached the finals of the Orange Bowl and the Pepsi Junior Masters, losing each time to Andrea Jaeger. That year she went on to be ranked inside the world's top 50 and is now inside the top 30. An all-rounder she won the Natal Super Sports Girl Award for eight sports.

Charlie Fancutt

Born: June 17, 1959, Brisbane, Australia.
Lives: Brisbane.
Height: 5–10. *Weight:* 165. Righthanded.
Career Highlights
Wimbledon: second round 1981.
Brisbane: quarter-finalist 1981.

Charlie blasted Ivan Lendl out of Wimbledon in the first round in 1981. His name hasn't been on the tip of many tongues since then though. Later in '81 he also reached the quarter finals of the Brisbane Tournament. Single.

John Feaver

Born: February 16, 1952, Fleet, Hampshire, England.
Lives: Wimbledon.
Height: 6–3. *Weight:* 175. Righthanded.

Charlie Fancutt.

Career Highlights
Wimbledon: last 16 1973.
U.S. Open: last 16 1977.
Davis Cup Team: 1977–'80.
Doubles
Nancy: finalist 1981 (with Hrebec).
Tel Aviv: finalist 1981 (with Krulevitz).
Bastad: finalist 1980 (with McNamara).
Palermo: finalist 1979 (with El Shafei).
Madrid: finalist 1979 (with R. Drysdale).

The big serving Feaver came close to defeating John Newcombe at Wimbledon in 1976 when he took the Australian to five sets, serving 42 aces on the way. Educated at Millfield, he reached the last 16 of Wimbledon in 1973 and the last 16 at the U.S. Open in 1977. He was arrested in Lagos in 1981 because he had played in South Africa. His highest British ranking was four in 1981. Married to Allison.

Peter Feigl

Born: November 30, 1951, Vienna, Austria.
Lives: Vienna.
Height: 6–0. *Weight:* 170. Righthanded.
Career Highlights
Australian Open: quarter-finalist 1979.
Italian Open: last 16, 1979.
Australian Indoor: quarter-finalist 1979.
Egyptian Open: champion 1979.
New Zealand Open: finalist 1979.
German Open: last 16 1979.

In 1978 Peter postponed law studies to turn pro and play tennis full-time and he has no reason to think he made a mistake. In his first Grand Prix tournament, at Cleveland, he fought his way though qualifying and won the title. He has also won events in such exotic locations at Lagos and Egypt, where in 1979 he beat Stan Smith. His best ranking was 45 in 1978 and he is now on his way down. Married to Uschi with a son, Florian.

Wojtek Fibak

Born: August 30, 1952, Poznan, Poland.
Lives: Poznan and New York, U.S.A.
Height: 6–0. *Weight:* 155.

Wojtek Fibak.

Righthanded.
Career Highlights
Wimbledon: quarter-finalist 1980; last 16 1981.
U.S. Open: quarter-finalist 1980.
French Open: quarter-finalist 1977, 1980; last 16 1981.
Masters: finalist 1976.
U.S. Pro Indoor: finalist 1981.
U.S. Clay Courts: finalist 1976.
U.S. Pro Championship: semi-finalist 1977.
Doubles
WCT World: champion 1976 (with Meller), 1978 (with Okker).
Australian Open: champion 1978 (with Warwick).
U.S. Pro Indoor: champion 1979 (with Okker).
U.S. National Indoor: champion 1979 (with Okker).

One of the most famous men in Poland, Fibak is a model ambassador for his country: intelligent, courteous, consistent and fluent in six languages. He first played when he was 13, became Poland's top junior and competed at junior Wimbledon in 1970. Professional sport, though, was forbidden in Poland and it was not until he reached the quarter finals of the Spanish Open in 1974 with wins over Ashe and Juan Gisbert that the Polish Federation relented and allowed him to play for cash.

He maintained his law studies at Mickiewicz University and completed his degree in 1979. A personal friend of Pope John Paul II, he calls at the Vatican for a coaching lesson each time he is in Rome. He has a superb collection of 18th century Polish art as well as canvases by the more modern masters. Friend and mentor to Ivan Lendl, Fibak also decided to duck Wimbledon in 1982. But he dropped into Wembley in November to KO Wilander in the Bensen and Hedges.

Now reaching the autumn of his career that saw him in the top 20 for six consecutive years, he plans to become a film director when he retires. Married to Ewa, with daughters Agnieszka and Paulinka.

Jaime Fillol

Born: June 3, 1946, Santiago, Chile.
Lives: Santiago.
Height: 5–11. *Weight:* 160.
Righthanded
Career Highlights
South African Open: semi-finalist 1972, 1973.
German Open: semi-finalist 1973, 1974.
Canadian Open: semi-finalist 1972.
U.S. Clay Courts: semi-finalist 1971.
Mexico City: champion 1981.
British Hard Courts: semi-finalist 1971.
Doubles
Wimbledon: semi-finalist 1972 (with Cornejo).
U.S. Open: finalist 1974 (with Cornejo).
French Open: finalist 1972 (with Cornejo).
Palermo: finalist 1981 (with Prajoux).
British Hard Courts: finalist 1971 (with Cornejo).

You'll never find this charming Chilean arguing on court – not for him the tantrums that so often spoil the game. He's played a major part in the players' own union – the ATP – and has always tried to stamp out the kind of histrionics that are becoming commonplace. He's setting up his own tennis club in Santiago to practise what he preaches. Married to Mindy, with son Jaime and daughters Cecilia, Natalia and Cataliana.

John Fitzgerald

Born: December 28, 1960, Cummins, South Australia.
Lives: Cummins.
Height: 6–1. *Weight:* 170. Righthanded.
Career Highlights
Wimbledon: last 16 1981.
Australian Indoor: semi-finalist 1981.
Kitzbuhel Grand Prix: champion 1981.
Davis Cup: semi-finalist 1981.

The new heartthrob of the tennis scene, Fitzgerald's outdoor boy good looks are in keeping with his rugged playing talent. As an unknown two years ago he surprised everyone by beating Fibak and Vilas to win the Kitzbuhel title in Austria. That helped the Australian jump 76 places on the world computer to No 60. He is currently ranked 40. Drafted into the Davis Cup team for the match with the United States in 1981, Fitzgerald suddenly collapsed during practice and was rushed to hospital. The illness was never completely diagnosed although it may have been a temporary fit. He was raised on his parents' 3,800 acre sheep farm, hence his nickname 'Country'. Single.

Peter Fleming

Born: January 21, 1955, Summit, New Jersey.
Lives: Seabrook Island, South Carolina.
Height: 6–5. *Weight:* 184. Righthanded.
Career Highlights
Wimbledon: quarter-finalist 1980.
Los Angeles: champion 1979.
ATP Championships: champion 1979.
WCT Challenge Cup: finalist 1979.
WCT Tournament of Champions: third place 1979.
Doubles

Peter Fleming.

Wimbledon: champion 1979, 1981 finalist 1982 (with McEnroe).
U.S. Open: champion 1979; 1981 finalist 1980 (with McEnroe).
WCT World Championships: champion 1979 (with McEnroe).
Masters: champion 1979 (with McEnroe).
Italian Open: champion 1979 (with Smid).

This 6ft 5in blond bombshell made a dramatic rise to world No 7 in 1979 and headed the doubles computer with his illustrious partner, John McEnroe. He started tennis at age five and had some early coaching from the Australian master, Harry Hopman, at his Port Washington Academy. He was a history major at UCLA and runner up in the 1976 NCAA Championships to Bill Scanlon. He turned professional in June 1976. His rise from 26 on the ATP computer ranking at the end of 1979, was triggered by outstanding performances to reach the final of the $320,000 WCT Challenge Cup in Montego Bay, Jamaica. He beat Borg, McEnroe and Stockton before losing a tough five-setter to Nastase in the final. Then it was on to London where he and McEnroe won the WCT Braniff World Doubles Championship . . . then back to New York for the Grand Prix Masters Doubles title. McEnroe and Fleming later won the Wimbledon and U.S. Open doubles titles . . . and Fleming joined with Tomas Smid to win the Italian Open. McEnroe was injured for the French Open, otherwise they might have been in line for a doubles 'Grand Slam'. He has since suffered a slump through injury. Married British model Jenifer Hudson in 1982.

Zeljko Franulovic

Born: June 13, 1947, Split, Yugoslavia.
Lives: Split.
Height: 6–1. *Weight:* 175. Righthanded.
Career Highlights
French Open: finalist 1970; semi-finalist 1971; quarter-finalist 1969.
U.S. Clay Courts: champion 1969, 1971.
Italian Open: quarter-finalist 1967.
Nice: quarter-finalist 1981.
Washington Star: quarter-finalist 1980.
Munich: quarter-finalist, 1980.
Cairo: quarter-finalist 1980.
Stuttgart: quarter-finalist 1980.
South American Open: champion 1969, 1977.

When it comes to Open tennis, you'd be forgiven if you didn't associate it with Franulovic, who is now past his prime. But the Yugoslavian was one of the prime movers in dragging the sport into modern times. He has a degree in law and is married to Nada, with a daughter Lana and son Denni.

Rod Frawley

Born: September 8, 1952, Brisbane, Australia.
Lives: Sydney, Australia and Berlin, West Germany.
Height: 6–1. *Weight:* 170. Righthanded.
Career Highlights
Wimbledon: semi-finalist 1981; last 32 1980.
Australian Open: quarter-finalist 1979; last 16 1981.
Davis Cup: semi-final 1980.
Doubles
New Zealand Open: champion 1980

Rod Frawley.

(with Feigl).
U.S. National Indoor: finalist 1980 (with Smid).
German Open: semi-finalist 1980 (with Slozil).

A typical Australian player with a fine serve-volley game, Frawley considered he was unable to make a living on the tour and 'retired' to concentrate on coaching in West Germany. But in 1976 he decided to return and in 1980 broke into the top 50. The following year his results were even more dramatic as he reached the semi-finals of Wimbledon before losing a hard match to McEnroe. Later in the year he beat Mark Edmondson in the Queensland Open and Roscoe Tanner in the Australian Open. His brother John, is one of Australia's best young prospects. Single.

Dianne Fromholtz.

Dianne Fromholtz

Born: August 10, 1956, Albury, Australia.
Lives: Elanora Heights, New South Wales.
Height: 5–4. *Weight:* 120. Lefthanded.
Career Highlights
Wimbledon: quarter-finalist 1979; last 16 1978, 1980.
U.S. Open: semi-finalist 1976; last 16, 1977, 1979, 1980.
French Open: semi-finalist 1979, 1980.
Australian Open: finalist 1977; semi-finalist 1975.
Wimbledon Plate: champion 1975.
Italian Open: semi-finalist 1975; quarter-finalist 1979.
U.S. Clay Courts: finalist 1975; semi-finalist 1974.
Canadian Open: semi-finalist 1975.
South African Open: finalist 1974.
Colgate Championships: fifth place tie 1977.
U.S. Indoor: finalist 1979, 1980; semi-finalist 1976.
Toyota Classic: champion 1978.
New South Wales Open: champion 1978.
Avon Championships: semi-finalist 1979.
Federation Cup – 1974–80.
Doubles
Australian Open: champion 1977.
Wimbledon Mixed: finalist 1980.

Reckoned to be the finest lefthanded woman player ever produced by Australia, the attractive Di has lost her sparkle in recent years after being ranked world No 4 in 1979. A typical outdoor Aussie who enjoys horse riding and cycling, Di also shone at the more artistic pursuit of ballet. But she eventually decided to concentrate on tennis and left school at 16 to join the globe-trotting circuit.

She entered the world top 10 in 1976 and in 1979 earned more than £100,000 in prize money. She was born two streets away from the great Margaret Court.

Bonnie Gadusek

Born: September 11, 1963, Pittsburg, Pennsylvania, U.S.A.
Lives: Key Largo, Florida.
Height: 5–6. *Weight:* 120. Righthanded.
Career Highlights
U.S. Open: last 16 1982.
French Open: third round 1982.
German Open: semi-finalist 1982.
Italian Open: quarter-finalist 1982.

Bonnie began her sports career as a gymnast and would have made the U.S. team had she not suffered an horrific injury in 1976 when she fell from the parallel bars onto her neck. She was in a full-body plaster for six months and doctors advised that another fall could kill her. Her family gave her a tennis racket instead and within three months of leaving hospital she was playing in her first tournament wearing a neck brace.

Bonnie combines her gymnast's grace with power and speed and made her mark on the Australian circuit in 1981 when she twice beat Dianne Fromholtz. In the 1982 German Open she beat Hana Mandlikova to reach the semi-finals.

Zina Garrison

Born: November 16, 1963, Houston, Texas, U.S.A.
Lives: Houston.
Height: 5–5. *Weight:* 130. Righthanded.
Career Highlights

Zina Garrison.

Wimbledon: last 16 1982; junior champion 1981.
French Open: quarter-finalist 1982.
Eastbourne: quarter-finalist 1982.
U.S. Junior: champion 1981.
U.S. Girls' 16s: champion 1980.

The youngest of seven children, Zina was discovered watching tennis coaching lessons in a public park near her home in Houston. She was invited to join in and showed an immediate talent for the sport. A fast, determined competitor with a busy all-court style, Zina is being touted as the greatest black player since Althea Gibson. She was presented with the International Tennis Federation's Junior of the Year Award for 1981, after winning the Wimbledon and U.S. Open junior titles.

Rolf Gehring

Born: November 25, 1955, Dusseldorf, West Germany.
Lives: Dusseldorf.
Height: 6–1. *Weight:* 175. Righthanded.
Career Highlights
French Open: last 16 1978.

A very experienced pro. He hit the headlines in 1981 by defeating Bjorn Borg in Brussels where he reached the semis. In the same year he also defeated José-Luis Clerc in the Davis Cup and Corrado Barazzutti in the Nations Cup for West Germany. He began playing tennis at the age of seven and is another player who likes clay, although he is keen to be good on all surfaces. His career has been restricted slightly because he has weak ankles and is prone to injury. Single.

Ruta Gerulaitis

Born: November 18, 1955, New York, U.S.A.
Lives: Kings Point, New York.
Height: 5–5½. *Weight:* 118. Righthanded.
Career Highlights
Wimbledon: last 16, 1978.
French Open: quarter-finalist 1979.
Westchester, New York WTA: finalist 1976.

Younger sister of Vitas, Ruta learned the sport from their father, Vitas Snr., who is teaching pro at Flushing Meadow. She joined the pro tour in 1976 and climbed to No 31 in the world in 1980 before being troubled by a shoulder injury. She enjoys water skiing and – like her brother – disco dancing. Of Lithuanian descent, she speaks fluent Lithuanian and French.

Vitas Gerulaitis

Born: July 26, 1954, Brooklyn, New York, U.S.A.
Lives: Kings Point, New York.
Height: 6–0. *Weight:* 160. Righthanded.
Career Highlights
Wimbledon: semi-finalist 1977, 1978.
U.S. Open: finalist 1979; semi-finalist 1978, 1981.
Australian Open: champion 1977.
Italian Open: champion 1977, 1979.
WCT Finals: champion 1978.
Doubles
Wimbledon: champion 1975 (with Sandy Mayer).

The already high-powered life of 'Broadway' Vitas took a controversial turn in 1982 when his name was mentioned in court during a cocaine drugs trial. One of the most flamboyant characters on the circuit, the non-drinking 'Lithuanian Lion' loves the disco scene. A member of the world's top ten since 1977, Vitas has always just fallen short of fulfilling his great

Vitas Gerulaitis.

potential. He has won the Italian Open, but otherwise the spectre of Bjorn Borg has always haunted him. It was Borg, his great friend, who beat him in an epic five-setter in the 1977 Wimbledon semi-final. Since then he has never beaten the Swede in crucial matches at Wimbledon and the U.S. Open.

An intense competitor with a fast, all-court game, Vitas went through a temperamental period of arguing with officials. He has also fallen out with the Press and invariably refuses to attend after-match interviews although he is fined by his union, ATP, each time. Single.

Sammy Giammalva

Born: March 24, 1963, Houston, Texas, U.S.A.
Lives: Houston.
Height: 5–10. *Weight:* 160. Righthanded.
Career Highlights
WCT Finals: quarter-finalist 1981.
Napa: champion 1981.
Cologne: semi-finalist 1981.
Swiss Indoor: quarter-finalist 1981.
U.S. National Junior: champion 1980.

Slight in stature, Sammy contains a real knockout in his powerful tennis shots. Son of former Davis Cup player Sammy Snr. and brother to touring pro Tony, he exploded onto the scene in 1981. An outstanding amateur, he couldn't wait to play for cash, but his father told him he could make the move only when he reached the world top 50. Wins over John Alexander and Hank Pfister, plus reaching the final of the WCT event in his home town of Houston, carried him way beyond that – to No 30. By way of a remarkable celebration, he was invited to play in the WCT Finals at Dallas as a late replacement for the injured Yannick Noah. Forgetting to cancel a date with his girlfriend, he jumped a plane to Dallas and lost bravely to Brian Gottfried. Single.

Sammy Giammalva.

Tony Giammalva

Born: April 21, 1958, Houston, Texas, U.S.A.
Lives: Houston.
Height: 6–3. *Weight:* 195. Righthanded.
Career Highlights
Wimbledon: last 32 1981.
French Open: last 32 1981.
Swedish Open: finalist 1980.
German Open: quarter-finalist 1981.

Son of Sammy Giammalva Snr. and brother of Sammy Jnr., Tony has all the background necessary to be a star. Dad was a member of the U.S. Davis Cup team in the Fifties and taught tennis in

Houston where his two boys were brought up. Tony turned pro in 1980 and by the end of the year was ranked 74 in the world. He is at his best on European clay courts, although his power game will soon suit grass.

Hans Gildemeister

Born: February 9, 1956, Lima, Peru.
Lives: Santiago, Chile.
Height: 6–0. *Weight:* 160.
Righthanded.
Career Highlights
French Open: quarter-finalist 1979, 1980.
German Open: quarter-finalist 1978.
Spanish Open: champion 1979.
U.S. Pro Championships: finalist 1979.

While players are jumping on the two-fisted shot bandwaggon Gildemeister thinks it's all child's play – literally! For when he was only five and began playing with his brother's racket back home in Chile, it was far too heavy and he had to use two hands to hold it: he has never changed his style since and he uses two hands on all his groundstrokes. Married to Margarita.

Angel Gimenez

Born: October 10, 1955, Barcelona, Spain.
Lives: Barcelona.
Height: 5–4. *Weight:* 135.
Righthanded.
Career Highlights
British Hard Courts: champion 1980.
Vienna: champion 1980.
Cairo: quarter-finalist 1981.
Nice: quarter-finalist 1981.
Hamburg: quarter-finalist 1981.
Boston: quarter-finalist 1981.
Davis Cup: 1977, 1979, 1980, 1981.
Kings Cup: 1975–1979.

Angel Gimenez.

Doubles
Hamburg: semi-finalist 1981 (with Velasco).
Bastad: semi-finalist 1980 (with Hocevar).

The righthander from Barcelona has always had an uphill battle because of his tiny 5ft 4in frame. But he more than makes up for his lack of height with a battling instinct that has surprised many a loftier opponent. A tireless, terrier of a player who is never without his lucky cap, he is still single.

Shlomo Glickstein

Born: January 6, 1958, Ashkelon, Israel.
Lives: Ashkelon.
Height: 6–2. *Weight:* 195. Righthanded.
Career Highlights
Wimbledon Plate: champion 1980.
Australian Hard Courts: champion 1980.
British Hard Courts: finalist 1980.
South Orange Grand Prix: champion 1981.
Canadian Open: semi-finalist 1981.
South African Open: semi-finalist 1981.

The son of Polish parents, Glickstein was born on the Mediterranean, some 30 miles from Tel Aviv at Ashkelon, the Biblical city where Samson killed himself by pulling the pillars of a house down on the Philistines. Glickstein spent three years in the Israeli Army and emerged, a strong, silent individual with a definite will of his own. He announced his presence in 1981 when he crashed into the world's top 50. Ended Richard Lewis' hopes at Wembley during the Benson and Hedges tournament in 1982. Single.

Andres Gomez

Born: March 15, 1960, Guayaquil, Ecuador.
Lives: Guayaquil.
Height: 6–5. *Weight:* 190. Lefthanded.
Career Highlights
Italian Open: champion 1982.
Bordeaux: champion 1981.
Santiago: finalist 1981.
Washington Star: semi-finalist 1981.
Madrid: semi-finalist 1981.
Quito: semi-finalist 1981.
Doubles
Italian Open: champion 1981 (with Gildemeister).
Bordeaux: champion 1981 (with Prajoux).
Brussels: champion 1981 (with Cano).
Hamburg: champion 1981 (with Gildemeister).
Madrid: champion 1981 (with Gildemeister).
Quito: champion 1981 (with Gildemeister).

Andres' mighty top spin forehand had gone close to causing upsets in 1981 when he lost in five sets to Lendl in the French Open and Connors at the U.S. Open. And in 1982 came the breakthrough he had threatened when he won the Italian Open title, beating Wilander in the semi-final and Teltscher in the final. Deceptively agile for a man of 6ft 5in, Gomez is determined to get as much out of his clay court game as possible before moving to grass. Single.

Francisco Gonzalez

Born: November 19, 1955, Wiesbaden, West Germany.
Lives: Ascuncion, Paraguay.
Height: 6–4. *Weight:* 195. Righthanded.

Career Highlights
Wimbledon: last 16 1981.
Cincinatti: finalist 1980.
San Juan: semi-finalist 1981.
Doubles
Tulsa: champion 1979 (with Teltscher); finalist 1980 (with Winitsky).
Sydney: champion 1979 (with Frawley).

Known on the circuit as The Cisco Kid, he is one of the most likeable guys around. The giant son of a U.S. Army Officer was born in Wiesbaden, West Germany, like John McEnroe. He started playing tennis when he was 11 and quickly proved he was a natural. He has been improving ever since. Married to Vivian.

Evonne Goolagong
see **Evonne Cawley**

Brian Gottfried

Born: January 27, 1952, Baltimore, Maryland, U.S.A.
Lives: Bonaventure, Florida.
Height: 6–0. *Weight:* 165. Righthanded.
Career Highlights
Wimbledon: semi-finalist 1980; quarter-finalist 1978.
U.S. Open: quarter-finalist 1977, 1978.
French Open: finalist 1977.
Italian Open: semi-finalist 1977.
WCT Finals: semi-finalist 1981; quarter-finalist 1978, 1979.
Davis Cup: champions 1978.
Doubles
Wimbledon: champion 1976 (with Ramirez); finalist 1979 (with Ramirez).
French Open: champion 1975, 1977 (with Ramirez).
Italian Open: champion 1974, 1975, 1976, 1977 (with Ramirez).
WCT World: champion 1975, 1980 (with Ramirez).

When you talk about devotion to duty you just have to mention Gottfried. This six foot workaholic surprised everyone when he actually missed a planned practice session to get married! But, sure enough, big Brian quickly made up for it in typical style by having two sessions the very next day. Brian has played tennis since he was old enough to hold a racket and after winning 14 junior titles at national level carried on progressing. He believes the turning point in his career came in 1976 when he had Borg on the verge of defeat in the U.S. Open but let him off. Married to Windy, with a son Kevin.

Brian Gottfried.

Tim Gullikson

Born: September 8, 1951, La Crosse, Wisconsin, U.S.A.
Lives: Boca Raton, Florida.
Height: 5–11. *Weight:* 175. Righthanded.
Career Highlights
Wimbledon: quarter-finalist 1979.
U.S. Open: last 16 1979.
French Open: last 16 1979.
South African Open: champion 1978.
U.S. National Indoor: finalist 1978.
Doubles
ATP Championship: finalist 1977 (with brother Tom), 1979 (with Carmichael).

The younger of the Gullikson twins by five minutes, Tim was a late starter in tennis, being voted 'Newcomer of the Year' in 1977 at the age of 26. The easy going righthander graduated in physical education from Northern Illinois University along with his brother – and then both married sisters from the same university. Tim coached at Dayton, Ohio, where fellow coach Hank Jungle persuaded him to have a crack at the circuit. In 1979 he was No 15 in the world. Son of a Wisconsin barber, Tim trimmed McEnroe down to size on Wimbledon's notorious No 2 court in 1979 when he reached the quarter-finals. Married to Rose.

Tom Gullikson

Born: September 8, 1951, La Crosse, Wisconsin, U.S.A.
Lives: Palm Coast, Florida.
Height: 5–11. *Weight:* 170. Lefthanded.
Career Highlights
U.S. National Indoor: semi-finalist 1977, 1981.
U.S. Open: quarter-finalist, 1982.

A victorious Tim Gullikson after beating McEnroe at Wimbledon.

Australian Indoor: quarter-finalist 1981.
South African Open: quarter-finalist 1981.
Tokyo Super Tennis: finalist 1980.
Doubles
ATP Championship: finalist 1977 (with brother Tim).

The lefthanded and elder of the Gullikson twins has not enjoyed as much success as his brother. But he has notched up career wins over Borg and Connors. Like Tim a late starter in tennis, Tom never played junior events. One of the nicest, most affable players on the circuit. Married, to Julie with daughters Petra and Christina.

Heinz Gunthardt

Born: February 8, 1959, Zurich, Switzerland.
Lives: Zurich.
Height: 5–10. *Weight:* 155. Righthanded.
Career Highlights
U.S. Pro Championships: last 16 1979.
Spanish Open: last 16 1979.
Wimbledon Junior: champion 1976.
French Open Junior: champion 1976.
Italian Open Junior: champion 1976.
Doubles
WCT World: champion 1982 (with Taroczy).

With a coach like Bob Hewitt, it's not surprising that Gunthardt is an exceptional doubles player. He has a lengthy list of doubles successes to his credit, already beginning with a Munich title playing with – Hewitt. He has a tremendous serve for a slender player and, as Hewitt says: '*He has all the shots of McEnroe but just lacks his drive.*' Single.

Heinz Gunthardt.

Barbara Hallquist

Born: May 1, 1957, Pasadena, California, U.S.A.
Lives: Arcadia, California.
Height: 5–8½. *Weight:* 142. Righthanded.
Career Highlights
U.S. Open: quarter-finalist 1980.
La Costa WTA: quarter-finalist 1979.
Women in Tennis Intl. (San Antonio): quarter-finalist 1978.
USTA College Nationals: champion 1976–77.
AIAW College Nationals: finalist 1977.
Doubles
U.S. Open: quarter-finals 1979, 1980 (with Desfor).
U.S. Clay Courts: quarter-finalist 1979, 1980 (with Desfor).
New South Wales: champion 1979 (with Desfor).

She caused the big shock of the 1980 U.S. Open by reaching the quarter-final, but is best known as a doubles player. With Diane Desfor, she reached third place on the U.S. doubles list in 1979.

Sylvia Hanika.

Sylvia Hanika

Born: November 30, 1959, Munich, West Germany.
Lives: Haar, West Germany.
Height: 5–7½. *Weight:* 128. Lefthanded.
Career Highlights
U.S. Open: quarter-finalist 1979, 1981.
French Open: finalist 1981.
Italian Open: finalist 1979.
German Open: semi-finalist 1978; quarter-finalist 1979.
Colgate International (Christchurch, New Zealand): finalist 1878.
Swedish Open: finalist 1978.
Austrian Open: finalist 1978, 1979, 1981.
Daihatsu Challenge Brighton: semi-finalist 1979, 1980.
German Indoor: champion 1978, 1979; finalist 1977.
Stockholm Open: semi-finalist 1980.
Swiss Open: finalist 1980.
Wimbledon Junior: semi-finalist 1977.
French Open Junior: semi-finalist 1977.
Federation Cup team: 1978–82.

Sylvia Hanika broke through in 1979 when she was voted the Most Improved Player of the tour. She reached the Italian Open final and the U.S. Open quarter-final. She defeated Dianne Fromholtz and Evonne Cawley on the way to the Italian final and followed that in 1981 by reaching the final of the French Open, where she lost to Hana Mandlikova. On the way, though, she had beaten Martina Navratilova in the quarter-finals to confirm herself as a feared adversary on clay. Daughter of a builder, she is powerfully built. A competition skier as a child, she also played midfield in the Munchengladbach women's soccer team.

Tanya Harford

Born: November 28, 1958, Cape Town, South Africa.
Lives: Johannesburg, South Africa.
Height: 5–3¾. *Weight:* 130. Righthanded.
Career Highlights
Wimbledon: last 32 1980.
South African Open: finalist 1979; quarter-finalist 1976.
Beckenham: semi-finalist 1979.
Beckenham Under 21: champion 1979.

Southwest African Open: champion 1977.
Irish Open: finalist 1976.
British Hard Court Under 21: champion 1978.
Orange Bowl: semi-finalist 1976.
Doubles
South African Open: champion 1978, 1979 (with Charles).

Never ranked in the top 30 but always regarded as a dangerous floater in any draw. She overcame injury in 1979 to beat Virginia Wade and reach the semi finals at Chichester. But her best result remains a place in the South African Open final in 1979. A free spirited, fun-loving girl who shuns the trappings of stardom. '*I say what I please and that upsets some of the girls*,' she admits. '*But I don't mind. It's only a game, isn't it?*'

José Higueras

Born: March 1, 1953, Granada, Spain.
Lives: Barcelona.
Height: 5–10. *Weight:* 163. Righthanded.
Career Highlights
French Open: quarter-finalist 1977, 1979.
German Open: champion 1979, 1982; last 16 1981.
Italian Open: last 16 1981.
U.S. Pro: champion 1979.
U.S. Clay Courts: semi-finalist 1979, 1980.

The bearded buccaneer has represented Spain in Davis Cup since 1973. A superb clay court player, he reached the semi-final of the Italian Open in 1978 and walked off court in his match with Panatta in protest against the gross crowd behaviour. Panatta had just saved four set points in recovering from 1–5 down to win the second set and level the match. One game earlier umpire Bertie Bowron had walked off as well.

An insomniac who relaxes during sleepless hours by reading and listening to music, José contracted hepatitis in 1980 soon after reaching the world's top ten and has never quite regained the slow court form which helped him to a place in the Masters Final of 1979. He led Spain to Galea Cup victory in 1973. Married to Donna.

Per Hjertquist

Born: April 6, 1960, Badafors, Sweden.
Lives: Stockholm, Sweden.
Height: 6–0. *Weight:* 160. Righthanded.
Career Highlights
Wimbledon Junior: semi-finalist 1978.

José Higueras.

U.S. Junior: champion 1978.
French Junior: finalist 1978.
Italian Junior: finalist 1978.
Pepsi World Junior: champion 1978.
Sofia: champion 1980.
Tel Aviv: finalist 1981.
Hilversum: quarter-finalist 1980.
Kitzbuhel: quarter-finalist 1981.
Brussels: quarter-finalist 1981.
Nations Cup team: 1981–82.
Doubles
Tel Aviv: champion 1980 (with Krulevitz).

It was after defeating Lendl to win the U.S. Open junior title in 1978 that people first started taking notice of Hjertquist. He gave up school at 16 to pursue his tennis career. With Wilander, he is among the exciting new Swedes following in Borg's footsteps.

Anne Hobbs.

Anne Hobbs

Born: August 21, 1959, Nottingham, Nottinghamshire, England.
Lives: London.
Height: 5–6. *Weight:* 120. Righthanded.
Career Highlights
Eastbourne: quarter-finalist 1978.
U.S. Indoor: quarter-finalist 1980.
South Australian Open: quarter-finalist 1978.
Wimbledon Plate: semi-finalist 1980; quarter-finalist 1978.
Colgate Intl. (Christchurch, New Zealand) quarter-finalist 1978.
Manchester: champion 1978, 1980.
Trophee Pernod of Bournemouth: champion 1977.
Trophee Pernod of Lee-on-Solent: champion 1980.
Wightman Cup team: 1978–80.
Federation Cup team: 1978–80.
Doubles
U.S. Open: quarter-finals 1978

When she beat Sue Barker at Manchester in 1978 it seemed she was on her way. But she has not quite been able to string together her undoubted talent. One of the fittest girls on the circuit, 'Hobbitt' has had outstanding success in the women's Superstars Competitions.

Marcos Hocevar

Born: September 25, 1955, Tjui, Brazil.
Lives: Porto Alegre, Brazil.
Height: 6–1. *Weight:* 185. Righthanded.
Career Highlights
Venice: semi-finalist 1981.
Gstaad: semi-finalist 1980.
Quito, Ecuador: semi-finalist 1980.

Nicknamed 'El Bruxo', the Magician, for some of his remarkable escapes on court. He has been on the pro circuit only four years and is considered one of the gentleman players. Showed his class by beating Adriano Panatta in Venice in 1981 despite the usual, partisan crowd.

Robert Van't Hof

Born: April 10, 1959, Lynwood, California, U.S.A.
Lives: Dallas, Texas.
Height: 6–4. *Weight:* 184. Righthanded.
Career Highlights
U.S. Amateur Indoors: champion 1978.
Hobart: finalist 1980.
Sarasota: quarter-finalist 1980.
NCAA: champion 1980.
Doubles
Tokyo: finalist 1981 (with Stefanki).

The lad from Lynwood, California, turned professional in 1980 and is now beginning to establish himself on the European circuit as a consistent player with a wide repertoire of shots. The former American Amateur Indoor champion is learning all the time.

Chip Hooper

Born: October 24, 1958, Washington D.C., U.S.A.
Lives: Sunnyvale, California.
Height: 6–6. *Weight:* 210. Righthanded.
Career Highlights
French Open: last 16 1982.
Queens Club: quarter-finalist 1982.
Rotterdam: quarter-finals 1982.
WCT Frankfurt: semi-finalist 1982.
U.S. Pro Indoor: semi-finalist 1982.
National College Indoors: champion 1981.
NCAA championships: quarter-finalist 1980, 1981.
Doubles
Winchester (England): champion 1977 (with Mel Purcell).

Chip Hooper.

Lawrence Barnett Hooper III is a giant chip off the ol' block who bludgeoned his way to stardom in the last week of January 1982. Then he not only qualified for the U.S. Pro Indoor Championships in Philadelphia but went on to the semi-finals with victories over Peter Fleming, Roscoe Tanner (the holder) and John Sadri before losing in four sets to Jimmy Connors.

His power game, with a serve timed at some 135 mph continued to impress in Europe as he blitzed Jimmy Arias in the French Open before falling to Connors again in the fourth round and a fortnight later at Wimbledon he dumped out the seeded Peter McNamara in the first round. Quite a performance for a young man who only two years earlier had been warned he may have to quit the sport because of a rare eye condition. The complaint, called pterygium, is an extreme sensitivity to bright sunlight, wind and dust which causes a film to develop over the eye. He twice needed delicate surgery and doctors warned him there was no guarantee he would see well enough to play top class tennis.

Surprisingly the 6ft 6in Chip was below average height at school and dwarfed by his towering brothers. His father, a Los Angeles surgeon, decided he should take up tennis and he was so successful that he won a tennis scholarship to Memphis State University.

Kathy Horvath.

Kathy Horvath

Born: August 25, 1965, Chicago, Illinois, U.S.A.
Lives: Hopewell Juncton, New York.
Height: 5–6½. *Weight:* 115. Righthanded.

Career Highlights
Wimbledon Junior: semi-finalist 1980.
French Open Junior: champion 1980.
Italian Open Junior: finalist 1980.
U.S. Girls' 18 Clay Courts: champion 1980.
Orange Bowl Junior International: champion 1980.
Pepsi Series Junior Championships: champion 1980.
U.S. Under 21: champion 1979.
U.S. Open Junior: semi-finalist 1979; quarter-finalist 1980.
U.S. Girls' 16's: champion 1979.
U.S. Amateur Clay Courts: finalist 1979.
U.S. Girls' 14 Clay Courts: champion 1978.
Maureen Connolly Junior Invitational: finalist 1979.
U.S. Girls' 12 Clay Courts: champion 1977.

Youngest ever winner of the U.S. Girls' 16 Nationals (13 yrs 11 months) and then in the following two weeks she became the youngest U.S. Under 21 champion, and the youngest to qualify for the U.S. Open. In 1980 she won the French Open Junior, reached the final of the Italian Open Junior and was a Wimbledon Junior semi-finalist. She lost in three sets to Kathy Rinaldi in the third round of the French Open in 1982 but, with Yvonne Vermaak, beat King and Kloss to take the Italian Open doubles title. Always elegant on court and a sporting opponent.

Jiri Hrebec

Born: September 19, 1950, Teplice, Czechoslovakia.
Lives: Prague, Czechoslovakia.
Height: 6–0. *Weight:* 175. Righthanded.
Career Highlights

Italian Open: quarter-finalist 1973.
German Open: quarter-finalist 1973.
Munich: semi-finalist 1979.
Cairo: quarter-finalist 1980.
Doubles
Nice: finalist 1980 (with Birner).
Nancy: finalist 1981 (with Feaver).

Hrebec is the fore-runner of the fine crop of Czechoslovak players now on the world scene like Lendl and Smid. Particularly good on slow courts, he is also a fine doubles player and was a member of his country's Davis Cup team. Married to Darina, with a daughter Andrea.

Andrea Jaeger

Born: June 4, 1965, Chicago, Illinois, U.S.A.
Lives: Lincolnshire, Illinois.
Height: 5–2½. *Weight:* 100. Righthanded.
Career Highlights
Wimbledon: quarter-finalist 1980.
U.S. Open: semi-finalist 1980, 1982.
French Open: finalist 1982.
U.S. Clay Courts: finalist 1980, champion, 1981.
Buick Riviera Classic (Las Vegas): champion 1980.
Maybelline Classic: finalist 1980.
Canadian Open: quarter-finalist 1980.
Beckenham: champion 1980.
Chichester: quarter-finalist 1980.
Orange Bowl International: champion 1979.
Pepsi Junior Masters: champion 1979.
Wightman Cup team: 1980.
Doubles
U.S. Open: semi-finalist 1980 (with Marsikova).

They call her 'Rocky' because of her competitive nature and because her Swiss-born father, Roland, is an ex-boxer. A real tomboy who played soccer and little league baseball, Andrea

Andrea Jaeger.

exploded onto the international scene in 1980 when she went through prequalifying to win the Avon Futures title in Las Vegas, a total of 13 matches.

She turned pro the following month aged 14 years and nine months, the youngest ever tour professional. Her first title as a member of the paid ranks was the 1980 Beckenham championship. That year she was the youngest player ever to be seeded at Wimbledon and went on to reach the quarter final. Two months later she battled through to the semi-final of the U.S. Open.

Her waist length hair was shorn early in 1982 to reveal a maturing young lady. She beat Chris Lloyd to reach the final of the French Open before falling in straight sets to Martina Navratilova. She was a surprise loser to Anne Smith in the fourth round of Wimbledon and went out to Chris Lloyd in the semi-final of the U.S. Open.

Susy Jaeger

Born: March 29, 1962, Chicago, Illinois, U.S.A.
Lives: Lincolnshire, Illinois.
Height: 5–6. *Weight:* 120. Righthanded.
Career Highlights
Easter Bowl Girls' 18s: champion 1979.
Rolex International Junior: champion 1978.
U.S. Under 21s: quarter-finalist 1978.
Doubles
U.S. Girls' 18: champion 1979 (with sister Andrea).

The elder sister of Andrea has not arrived with the same sort of impact but has made steady progress. She was ranked no 2 in U.S. junior doubles with little sister in 1979. She studied economics at Stanford University.

Andrew Jarrett

Born: January 9, 1958, Belper, Derbyshire, England.
Lives: Surrey.
Height: 6–0. *Weight:* 165. Righthanded.
Career Highlights
British Junior: champion 1976.
Auckland: semi-finalist 1979.
Gstaad: semi-finalist 1980; quarter-finalist 1981.
Quito: semi-finalist 1980.
Bogota: quarter-finalist 1980.
BP Cup team: 1978.

Andrew Jarrett.

Doubles
Auckland: finalist 1979 (with J. Smith).
Nancy: finalist 1979 (with R. Drysdale).
Paris Indoor: finalist 1981 (J. Smith).

Andrew was ranked in the top ten doubles teams in the world with Jonathon Smith at the start of 1982 after good wins in Australia and New Zealand. He is a permanent fixture in the Davis Cup and Kings Cup teams for Britain in doubles. His best ever singles finish was a semi-final spot in Auckland in 1979 and his highest position on the computer was 140 in 1978. Engaged to Debbie Jevans.

Mima Jausovec.

Anders Jarryd

Born: July 13, 1961, Lidkoping, Sweden.
Lives: Lidkoping.
Height: 5–11. *Weight:* 155. Righthanded.
Career Highlights
Bastad: finalist 1981.
Sweden National champion 1981.
Doubles
Linz: champion 1981 (with Simonsson).
Barcelona: champion 1981 (with Simonsson).
Bastad: finalist 1981 (with Simonsson).
Bordeaux: finalist 1981 (with Gurfein).

An accomplished doubles player, he is an important member of the Swedish Davis Cup team and wears spectacles on court. He has pushed his ranking quietly down into double figures without achieving any world shattering results. Single.

Mima Jausovec

Born: July 20, 1956, Maribor, Yugoslavia.
Lives: Maribor.
Height: 5–3. *Weight:* 110. Righthanded.
Career Highlights
Wimbledon: quarter-finalist 1978, 1981.
U.S. Open: semi-finalist 1976; quarter-finalist 1977, 1980.
French Open: champion 1977; finalist 1978.
Italian Open: champion 1976; semi-finalist 1975.
German Open: champion 1978;

Debbie Jevans

semi-finalist 1974–76.
Canadian Open: champion 1976.
Daihatsu Challenge (Brighton): finalist 1981.
Wimbledon Junior: champion 1974.
U.S. Open Junior: finalist 1974.
Federation Cup team: 1973, 1975, 1976, 1978, 1980, 1981, 1982.

Doubles
Wimbledon: finalist 1978 (with Ruzici).
U.S. Open: semi-finals 1976 (with Ruzici).
French Open: champion 1978 (with Ruzici).
Italian Open: finalist 1978 (with Ruzici).
German Open: champion 1978 (with Ruzici).

If injury had not plagued her career she might have been an even bigger name. She won the Italian Open in 1976, the French the following year and the German Open a year later. Her highest ranking was 9th in 1977 and, paired with Virginia Ruzici, she won the German, French and Italian doubles titles in 1978. A fine soccer player, she learnt to ski at the age of three. She studied economics at the University of Maribor.

Deborah Jevans

Born: May 20, 1960, London, England.
Lives: Seaford, Sussex.
Height: 5–6½. *Weight:* 135. Righthanded.

Career Highlights
Wimbledon: last 16, 1979.
Stockholm Open: finalist 1978.
Beckenham Under 21: finalist 1979.
Trophee Pernod Sutton: champion 1979.
British Junior Grass Courts: semi-finalist 1978.
Trophee Pernod Bournemouth: champion 1977.
Wightman Cup team: 1979–82.
Doubles
Beckenham: champion 1979 (with Durie).

Debbie left school in the summer of 1976 to concentrate on a full-time tennis career. In 1977 she won the Junior Wimbledon Championships, beating Kate Glancy in the final. She toured America with Jo Durie, representing Great Britain in the Continental Cup and the Orange Bowl. She reached the last 16 at Wimbledon in 1979 before losing to Virginia Wade. She made her Wightman Cup debut and has remained ever since as a doubles player with Durie. Engaged to fellow international Andrew Jarrett.

Kjell Johannson

Born: February 12, 1951, Delasjofors, Sweden.
Lives: Uppsala, Sweden.
Height: 5–9. *Weight:* 160. Righthanded.
Career Highlights
Lagos: champion 1978.
Biarritz: finalist 1979.
Bastad: semi-finalist 1979.
Vina del Mar: semi-finalist 1981.
Mar del Plata: quarter-finalist 1981.

He doesn't play much on the circuit nowadays. His best year was 1978 when he reached 51 on the computer. He also appeared in the Swedish Davis Cup team in the 1970's and has a Cup win over Balazs Taroczy. Married to Else-Mari.

Chris Johnstone

Born: October 12, 1960, Perth, Australia.
Lives: Perth.
Height: 5–9. *Weight:* 150. Righthanded.
Career Highlights
Melbourne: semi-finalist 1981.
Adelaide: quarter-finalist 1981.

A much improved player, he had a good win over Roscoe Tanner in Australia at the NSW Open in 1981. He definitely favours grass and did well at Wimbledon in 1982, reaching the third round before going out to British No 1 Buster Mottram. From 555 in the world in 1978, he has climbed into the top 100. Single.

Christiane Jolissaint

Born: December 9, 1961, Vevey, Switzerland.
Lives: Beinne, Switzerland.
Height: 5–7½. *Weight:* 145. Righthanded.
Career Highlights
Italian Open: third round 1980.
Avon Futures of Calgary: finalist 1980.
Avon Championships of Detroit: third round 1980.
Merseyside Championships: champion 1979.
Spanish Open: finalist 1978.
Chichester: third round 1980.
Berne, Switzerland: finalist 1979.
Swiss Junior: champion 1976.
Swiss National Championships: finalist 1977.
Annie Soisbault Cup team: 1978.
Federation Cup team: 1979–80.

Christiane Jolissaint jumped 126 places in six months in 1981, thanks to reaching the third round of the Italian Open and the Wimbledon Plate. Now she is ranked in the top 50. She was Swiss Junior champion and fifth ranked adult player in 1976, while still 14.

Barbara Jordan

Born: April 2, 1957, Milwaukee, Wisconsin, U.S.A.
Lives: King of Prussia, Pennsylvania.
Height: 5–5. *Weight:* 125. Righthanded.
Career Highlights
Wimbledon: last 32 1980.
Australian Open: champion 1980.
Sunbird Cup: semi-finalist 1980.
U.S. Under 21 National: champion 1978.
U.S. Under 21 Hard Courts: champion 1978.
USTA College Nationals: finalist 1978.

Created the shock of the 1980 season when she won the Australian Open, beating Hana Mandlikova, Renata Tomanova and finally Sharon Walsh to win 10,000 dollars, almost a third of the money she won that year. She has since been overshadowed by her more famous sister, Kathy. She has been deeply involved in committee work with the Women's Tennis Association.

Kathy Jordan

Born: December 3, 1959, Bryn Mawr, Pennsylvania, U.S.A.
Lives: King of Prussia, Pennsylvania.
Height: 5–8. *Weight:* 130. Righthanded.
Career Highlights
Wimbledon: last 16 1979, 1980, 1981.
U.S. Open: last 16 1979, 1980, 1981.
French Open: quarter-finalist 1980.

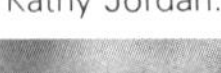

Kathy Jordan.

Canadian Open: semi-finalist 1980.
Avon Futures: champion 1979.
Family Circle Cup: quarter-finalist 1980.
AIAW College Nationals: champion 1979.
Wightman Cup team: 1979, 1980.
Federation Cup team: 1980, 1981, 1982.
Doubles
Wimbledon: champion 1980 (with Smith); finalist 1982.
U.S. Open: semi-finalist 1980 (with Smith).
French Open: champion 1980 (with Smith).

She was the doubles partner of Anne Smith when they won the Wimbledon and French titles in 1980 and has been a member of the U.S. Wightman and Federation Cup teams. The younger sister of Barbara, she has eclipsed big sister with wins over most of the top players including Tracy Austin and Virginia Wade. She is excitable and volatile on court although she insists she is trying to curb her temperament.

Billie Jean King (née Moffitt)

Born: November 22, 1943, Long Beach, California, U.S.A.
Lives: New York.
Height: 5–4½. *Weight:* 134. Righthanded.
Career Highlights
Wimbledon: champion 1966–68, 1972–73, 1975; finalist 1963, 1969–70.
U.S. Open: champion 1967, 1971–72, 1974; finalist 1965, 1968.
Australian Open: champion 1968; finalist 1969.
French Open: champion 1972.
Italian Open: champion 1970.
Virginia Slims circuit events: 29 titles 1970–78.
South African Open: champion 1966–67, 1969.
U.S. Indoor: champion 1966–68, 1971, 1974.
German Open: champion 1971.
Wightman Cup team: 1961–67, 1970, 1977–78.
Federation Cup team: 1963–67, 1976–79.
Doubles
Wimbledon: champion 1961 with Hantze), 1962 (with Susman), 1965 (with Bueno), 1967–68, 1970–71 (with Casals), 1972 (with Stove), 1973 (with Casals), 1979 (with Navratilova).
U.S. Open: champion 1964 (with Susman), 1967, 1974 (with Casals) 1978, 1980 (with Navratilova).
French Open: champion 1972 (with Stove).
Italian Open: champion 1970 (with Casals).
Wimbledon Mixed: champion 1967, 1971, 1973, 1974 (with Davidson).
U.S. Mixed: champion 1967, 1971, 1973 (with Davidson), 1976 (with Dent).

The great Billie Jean King must be the best known woman player of all time. She bounced into big time tennis as Billie Jean Moffitt in the 1960's before marrying Larry King in 1965, and has revolutionised the women's game ever since. Almost all the improvements must be down to her, although her personal publicity has suffered of late.

She has collected 20 Wimbledon titles – a record – and every other major championship. She was ranked No 1 in the U.S.A. seven times, equalling Molla Mallory and Helen Wills Moody, and has been in the U.S. Top 10 since she was 17 in 1960. A series of three knee

Billie Jean King.

operations followed by one on her ankle failed to kill her competitive spirit.

Carlos Kirmayr

Born: Spetember 23, 1950, Sao Paulo, Brazil.
Lives: Sao Paulo.
Height: 5–8. *Weight:* 150.
Righthanded.
Career Highlights
Wimbledon: last 32 1981.
French Open: last 16 1981.
WCT Tournament of Champions: finalist 1981.
Bogota: finalist 1980.
Kitzbuhel: semi-finalist 1980.
Johannesburg: semi-finalist 1980.
Gstaad: semi-finalist 1981.
Vienna: quarter-finalist 1981.
Doubles
Bogota: champion 1980 (with A. Fillol).
Brussels: finalist 1981 (with Motta).

Kirmayr was 26 before he started taking his tennis seriously. Now, at the age of 32, he is going through the best period of his career. Born in Brazil and educated in America, Kirmayr used tennis merely as relaxation from his first love – music. He was a drummer in several bands back in Sao Paulo until his last group, 'Os Pulgentos' – 'The Fleabags' – made hit rock records.

Ann Kiyomura

Born: August 22, 1955, San Mateo, California, U.S.A.
Lives: Mountain View, California.
Height: 5–1. *Weight:* 120. Righthanded.
Career Highlights
Avon Championships of Oakland: semi-finalist 1979.
Toray Sillook (Tokyo): semi-finalist 1979.
Japan Open: champion 1978, finalist 1975.
Wimbledon Junior: champion 1973.
Wightman Cup team: 1976, 1979.
Doubles
Wimbledon: champion 1975 (with Sawamatsu).
U.S. Open: semi-finalist 1976 (with Guerrant).

One of the world's great doubles partners, she and Kazuko Sawamatsu teamed up in 1975 to win Wimbledon and the Japanese Open. She is often partnered by British No 1 Sue Barker, with whom she has reached several finals.

Ann Kiyomura.

Johan Kriek.

Johan Kriek

Born: April 5, 1958, Pongola, South Africa.
Lives: Naples, Florida, U.S.A.
Height: 5–8. *Weight:* 155. Righthanded.
Career Highlights
Wimbledon: quarter-finalist 1981, 1982.
U.S. Open: quarter-finalist 1978, 1979.
WCT Finals: finalist 1981.
Australian Open: champion 1981, 1982.

A former star schoolboy rugby half back, Kriek is fast in every aspect of his play. Lightning serves, exceptionally quick returns – devastatingly swift about court. He left his native South Africa after a row with his federation.

The best seems yet to come from the player who has already been compared to Vitas Gerulaitis because of that tremendous speed. Big events always seem to bring out the best in him although he needs to watch his temperament.

Ramesh Krishnan

Born: June 5, 1961, Madras, India.
Lives: Madras.
Height: 5–7. *Weight:* 150.
Righthanded.
Career Highlights
U.S. Open: quarter-finalist 1981.
Montreal: quarter-finalist 1981.
Auckland: quarter-finalist 1979.
Cleveland: quarter-finalist 1979.
Wimbledon Junior: champion 1979.
French Junior: champion 1979.

His game contains an impressive array of shots and he has pulled off a list of big wins already, including victories over Stan Smith and Gene Mayer. He beat them on his way to the quarters of the U.S. Open in 1981. He followed in the footsteps of his father, Ramanathan, by playing Davis Cup for India. The highlights of his amateur career were the junior title wins at both the French and Wimbledon championships in 1979. Single.

Paul Kronk

Born: September 22, 1954, Queensland, Australia.
Lives: Calvundra, Australia.
Height: 6–2. *Weight:* 190.
Righthanded.
Career Highlights
Wimbledon: last 16 1981.
Doubles
U.S. Open: finalist 1976 (with Letcher).
San Juan: champion 1980 (with McNamee).
Melbourne: champion 1981 (with McNamara).
Vina del Mar: champion 1981 (with Carter). Mar del Plata: champion 1981 (with Carter).
Munich: champion 1981 (with Carter).
Kitzbuhel: champion 1981 (with Carter).

Big-serving Aussie Paul Kronk is another member of the powerful breed of doubles players to emerge from that country. He showed his promise back in 1976 when he reached the U.S. final with Cliff Letcher, but then lost a lot of ground because of back trouble.

Steve Krulevitz

Born: May 30, 1951, Baltimore, Maryland, U.S.A.
Lives: Washington D.C.
Height: 5–9. *Weight:* 155.
Righthanded.
Career Highlights
Italian Open: quarter-finalist 1974.
Mexico City: semi-finalist 1981.
Brussels: semi-finalist 1981.
Tel Aviv: semi-finalist 1981.
Basle: quarter-finalist 1981.
Doubles
Brussels: champion 1980 (with Stevaux).
Tel Aviv: champion 1980 (with Hjertquist); finalist 1981 (with Feaver).

Krulevitz was born in Baltimore but has Israeli parents and is therefore a member of their Davis Cup team, along with Schlomo Glickstein. He also has the distinction of having played on the U.S. Junior Davis Cup team in 1969. He reached the quarter-finals of the Italian Open in 1974. Married to Ann.

Iris Riedel Kuhn

Born: March 16, 1954, Sao Paulo, Brazil.
Lives: Berlin, West Germany.
Height: 5–6. *Weight:* 110.
Righthanded.
Career Highlights
German Open: semi-finalist 1975; quarter-finalist 1976–77.

U.S. Clay Courts: semi-finalist 1977, quarter-finalist 1975.
British Hard Courts: champion 1978.
Italian Open: quarter-finalist 1977, 1979.
Austrian Open: quarter-finalist 1977.
Spanish Open: finalist 1975, semi-finalist 1978.
Egyptian Championships: finalist 1975.
Federation Cup: 1972 (Brazil), 1976, 1978–1982 (West Germany).

Iris Riedel Kuhn was born in Brazil but moved to West Germany in 1973. She played for Brazil in the Federation Cup in 1972 and Germany in 1976. She won the British Hard Courts at Bournemouth in 1978 to halt a drop from 28 to 139 in the ranking and next year was a quarter-finalist in Rome, beating Rosie Casals and Virginia Wade.

Kate Latham

Born: October 25, 1952, San Francisco, California, U.S.A.
Lives: Palo Alto, California.
Height: 5–6. *Weight:* 125. Righthanded.
Career Highlights
Wimbledon Plate: semi-finalist 1979.
Phoenix Thunderbird Classic: semi-finalist 1979.
Virginia Slims of Houston: quarter-finalist 1974.
U.S. Clay Courts: quarter-finalist 1978.
Eastbourne: quarter-finalist 1974.
Central Fidelity Intl. (Richmond, Va): quarter-finalist 1979.
Manchester: champion 1974.
Beckenham: finalist 1974.
Crossley Carpets Trophy (Chichester): quarter-finalist 1979.

As head of the WTA disciplinary committee she cannot afford any John McEnroe tantrums. Congenital knee trouble which needed surgery has kept her off the tour for almost two years. A distant relative of Mark Twain, she was once a champion swimmer and is now an expert guitarist.

Andrea Leand

Born: January 18, 1964, Baltimore, Maryland, U.S.A.
Lives: Brooklandville, Maryland.
Height: 5–8. *Weight:* 132. Righthanded
Career Highlights
U.S. Open: last 16 1981.
French Open: last 16 1982.
U.S. Girls' 16s: finalist 1980.
U.S. Girls' 18s indoors: champion 1981.
Avon of Boston: semi-finalist 1982.

A sporting all-rounder at Bryn Mawr Academy in Baltimore where she played hockey and basketball as well as tennis, the tall, well-built Andrea rocketed into the limelight during the 1981 U.S. Open. Then she beat Renee Richards in the opening round, before KO'ing No 2 seed, Andrea Jaeger, and Julie Harrington to reach the last 16. She finally lost to Barbara Potter in three sets. In 1982 Andrea proved she was here to stay by battling through to the fourth round of the French Open. Single.

Henri Le Conte

Born: July 4, 1963, Lillers, France.
Lives: Paris.
Height: 6–1. *Weight:* 160. Lefthanded.
Career Highlights
French Junior: champion 1980.
Doubles
Bologna: champion 1981 (with S. Giammalva).

A promising French teenager, he has made progress in the shadow of Thierry Tulasne. He partners Ilie Nastase in doubles from time to time, so at least he can say he has had some fun. He won the French Open junior title in 1980. Single.

Ivan Lendl

Born: March 7, 1960, Ostrava, Czechoslovakia.
Lives: Ostrava.
Height: 6–2. *Weight:* 175. Righthanded.
Career Highlights
U.S. Open: finalist 1982.
French Open: finalist 1981.
Masters: finalist 1980; champion, 1982.

Ivan Lendl.

WCT Finals: champion 1982; semi-finalist 1980.
WCT Tournament of Champions: champion 1982.
Canadian Open: champion 1980, 1981.
Spanish Open: champion 1980, 1981.
South American Open: champion 1981.
Italian Open: semi-finalist 1981.
German Open: semi-finalist 1980.
U.S. Clay Courts: finalist 1981.
U.S. Open: quarter-finalist 1980.
Davis Cup: champions 1980.
Nations Cup: champions 1981.
Wimbledon: junior champion 1978.
French: junior champion 1978.
Italian: junior champion 1978.

The Czechoslovak iron man will be hoping to lose his 'nearly' tag in 1983. A phenomenal run of victories, particularly on the WCT circuit, brought him earnings of more than a million dollars in 1982, but the big titles still eluded him.

Grim and unsmiling on court, Lendl has gained a reputation for brusqueness off it. But his friends say this is undeserved; that he is witty, charming company and likes simply to preserve his privacy.

Lendl was the world's top junior in 1978, winning the Italian, French and Wimbledon titles. In his first full year as a pro, 1979, he finished No 20 in the world. He comes from a sporting family. His father, Jiri, a lawyer, was ranked in the Czech top 15 and his mother Olga was national No 2. His father is also a fine chess player, which might explain Lendl's intense, icy concentration.

In 1982 Lendl culminated his WCT plundering by beating McEnroe in the Dallas Finals and then moving to New York the following week to claim the Forest Hills Tournament of Champions. He had been beaten by Borg in five sets in Paris in 1981 and was confidently expected to go one better this time. But he lost to the sensational Matts Wilander in the fourth round.

Like his close friend and adviser, Wojtek Fibak, Lendl curiously chose to opt out of Wimbledon. He gained revenge over Wilander in the U.S. Open, but then ran into the rejuvenated Jimmy Connors in the final. He also suffered defeats against Borg in Australia later in the year when the Swede returned to the tour.

Sue Leo

Born: August 10, 1962, Brisbane, Queensland, Australia.
Lives: Stafford, Queensland.
Height: 5–4½. *Weight:* 125. Righthanded.
Career Highlights
Western Australian Open: champion 1980.
Queensland Open: champion 1976.
Toyota Mornington: finalist 1979.
Silverwater Classic: finalist 1979.
Australian Satellite Circuit Masters: finalist 1979.
South Australian Open: quarter-finalist 1979.
Pepsi Junior Masters: finalist 1980.
Wimbledon Junior: finalist 1980; semi-finalist 1979.
Australian Junior: finalist 1978.
U.S. Girls 18 Clay Courts: semi-finalist 1979.
B.P. Pepsi Bowl: semi-finalist 1979.
Federation Cup: 1980.

Sue won the Queensland Open in 1976, at the tender age of 14, to burst into the big time. She is a fine backgammon player and a good tactician on court.

Cliff Letcher

Born: February 9, 1952, Pyramid Hill, Australia.
Lives: Victoria, Australia.
Height: 6–0. *Weight:* 180. Righthanded.
Career Highlights
Australian Junior: champion 1971.
Caxton: quarter-finalist 1980.
Doubles
U.S. Open: finalist 1976 (with Kronk).
Australian Open: finalist 1978, 1979 (with Kronk).

Another in a long line of good Aussie doubles players. He was runner up at the U.S. Open with Paul Kronk in 1976. Two years later they reached the final of the Australian Open and repeated that feat the following year. He spends much of his time away from the circuit now. His best year was 1977 when his singles ranking peaked at 65. Married to Kathy.

Chris Lewis

Born: March 9, 1957, Auckland, New Zealand.
Lives: Auckland and Key Largo, Florida, U.S.A.
Height: 5–11. *Weight:* 155. Righthanded.
Career Highlights
ATP Championship: finalist 1981.
Munich Grand Prix: champion 1981.
Wimbledon: junior champion 1975.
U.S. Open: junior finalist 1975.
Davis Cup player since 1975.

The New Zealander helped knock Britain out of the Davis Cup in 1982 to confirm his position as their No. 1 player. He hates flying but still gets around and, since becoming the world's top junior player in 1975 has steadily improved. Single.

Richard Lewis

Born: December 6, 1954, Winchmore Hill, London, England.
Lives: Winchmore Hill.
Height: 6–3. *Weight:* 180. Lefthanded.
Career Highlights
New Zealand Open: champion 1976.
Auckland: semi-finalist 1979.
Paris Indoor: quarter-finalist 1981.
National Junior Grass Courts: champion 1972.
Davis Cup team: 1977, 1978, 1981, 1982.

The tall, fair-haired lefthander, ranked No 2 in Britain in 1982, travelled extensively in the early days of his career and won the New Zealand Open in 1976. He played an important role in Britain's Davis Cup run to the semi-finals in 1981 with victories over Italy and New Zealand.

Chris Evert Lloyd

Born: December 21, 1954, Fort Lauderdale, Florida.
Lives: Fort Lauderdale and Kingston, Surrey, England.
Height: 5–5½. *Weight:* 125. Righthand.
Career Highlights
Wimbledon: champion 1974, 1976, 1981; finalist 1973, 1978, 1979, 1980, 1982; semi-finalist 1972, 1975, 1977.
U.S. Open: champion 1975–78, 1980, 1982; finalist 1979; semi-finalist 1971–74.
Australian Open: champion 1982; finalist 1974, 1981.
French Open: champion 1974–75, 1979–80, finalist 1973, 1982.
Colgate Series Championships: champion 1977–78; third place 1979.
Virginia Slims Championships: champion 1977–73, 1975, 1977.

Chris Evert Lloyd.

Virginia Slims Circuit events: 23 from 1971–78.
Italian Open: champion 1974–75, 1980, 1981; finalist 1973.
U.S. Clay Courts: champion 1972–1975, 1979–80.
South African Open: champion 1973.
Canadian Open: champion 1974, 1980.
U.S. Indoor: champion 1978.
Family Circle Cup: champion 1974–78.
Eastbourne: champion 1974, 1976, 1979.
Chichester: champion 1980.
Wightman Cup team: 1971–73, 1975, 1977, 1982.
Federation Cup team: 1977–82.
Doubles
Wimbledon: champion 1976 (with Navratilova).
French: champion 1974 (with Morozova), 1975 (with Navratilova).
Italian: champion 1974 (with Morozova), 1975 (with Navratilova).

They called her 'Little Miss Icicle' when she won her first Wimbledon title as a 19-year-old. Her implaccable temperament and extreme concentration masked a warm, humorous person, who was only truly revealed to her public when she married British Davis Cup player John Lloyd on April 17, 1979.

Chris learned her mental toughness from her father Jim, a teaching pro at Fort Lauderdale, who was ranked No 11 in the U.S.A. in 1943. She turned pro on her 18th birthday, having declined more than 50,000 dollars in prize money that season to maintain her amateur status. She played World Team Tennis in 1976 for Phoenix Racquets and in 1978 for Los Angeles Strings. At the end of 1976 she was elected Sportswoman of the Year by Sports Illustrated and chosen as world champion by the International Tennis Federation in 1978, 1980 and 1981.

Earnings from her career so far are

Chris Evert Lloyd.

estimated at 8 million dollars. She was briefly eclipsed at the start of the Eighties by Martina Navrãtilova but returned in 1981 to reclaim her world No 1 spot in sensational style. Throughout that season she lost only six of 78 matches and stormed to the Wimbledon title she had set her heart on regaining without losing a set – the first woman to achieve that since the advent of Open tennis in 1968.

Her 56 match win streak in 1974 is a modern record for women and she also holds the record for the most consecutive wins on one surface with her 125 on clay, from August 1973 to May 1979, before losing to Austin in the semi-finals of the Italian Open. When she won her fourth consecutive U.S. Open in 1978, it equalled the record held by Molla Mallory (1915–18) and Helen Jacobs (1932–35). Her five consecutive years ranked as U.S. No 1 (1974–78) equalled the record held by Alice Marble (1936–49). The Australian Open was the only major title to have eluded her until she won that in 1982, beating Natratilova.

She is unbeaten in Wightman Cup and Federation Cup singles, a run of more than 40 matches. Her sister Jeanne was a tour pro until retiring in 1979 and her youngest sister Clare won the Under 12 division in the 1979 Orange Bowl. She also has two brothers, Drew and John.

John Lloyd

Born: August 27, 1954, Leigh-on-Sea, Essex, England.
Lives: Fort Lauderdale, Florida, U.S.A. and Kingston, Surrey.
Height: 5–10. *Weight:* 165.
Righthanded.
Career Highlights
Australian Open: finalist 1977.

John Lloyd.

Davis Cup: final 1978.
Doubles
French Open Mixed: champion 1982 with Turnbull.

'Legs' Lloyd the girl fans called him before he broke their hearts by going off and marrying women's tennis queen Chris Evert in Florida. His romance contributed to his slide from the World top 20 in 1977 – when he lost the final of the Australian Open to Gerulaitis – to outside the top 200. One of three tennis playing brothers – David is older and Tony younger – John was a driving force in the British Davis Cup team which reached the final against the U.S.A. in Palm Springs in 1978. He showed signs of a return to form last season with a couple of good wins at the French Open.

Jose Lopez-Maeso

Born: December 24, 1956, Puertollano, Spain.
Lives: Madrid, Spain.
Height: 5–8. *Weight:* 148. Righthanded.
Career Highlights
Mar del Plata: semi-finalist 1981.
Nancy: semi-finalist 1981.
Madrid: semi-finalist 1981.
Davis Cup team: 1981.

Jose's best win was over Roscoe Tanner in North Conway in 1981. He is also a Spanish Davis Cup player and another clay-court specialist. Single.

Peanut Louie

Born: August 15, 1960, San Francisco, California, U.S.A.
Lives: San Francisco.
Height: 5–5. *Weight:* 115. Righthanded.
Career Highlights
Borden Classic (Nagoya, Japan): semi-finalist 1980.
Avon Futures: semi-finalist 1980.
Wimbledon Junior: finalist 1977; semi-finalist 1978.
U.S. Girls' 18s: semi-finalist 1977–78.
U.S. Girls' 18 Hard Courts: champion 1976–1977; finalist 1978.
U.S. Girls' 18 Clay Courts: finalist 1977; semi-finalist 1978.
Bonne Bell Cup team: 1977–78.

Her real name is Mareen but she was the youngest of five children, so the nickname stuck – to the delight of the commentators. She burst onto the circuit in 1977 but suffered a loss of form that brought just eight wins in 29 matches from the 1978 U.S. Open to September of 1979.

Peanut Louie.

Fernando Luna

Born: April 24, 1958, Cuidad Real, Spain.
Lives: Barcelona, Spain.
Height: 5–9. *Weight:* 155. Righthanded.
Career Highlights
Orange Bowl: champion 1975.
European Junior: champion 1976.
Bastad: semi-finalist 1981.
Bordeaux: semi-finalist 1981.
Munich: quarter-finalist 1981.
Kitzbuhel: quarter-finalist 1981.
Nice: semi-finalist 1980.
Spanish Nationals: champion 1977, 1980.
Brussels: quarter-finalist 1980.
Davis Cup team: 1979, 1980.

A European Junior winner in 1976, Luna loves to play on clay where he has recorded his best win, over Eliot Teltscher in Munich in 1981. He has been a member of the Spanish Davis and Nations Cup teams and has gradually moved into the top 50. One to watch, but not on grass. Single.

Bob Lutz

Born: August 29, 1947, Lancaster, Pennsylvania, U.S.A.
Lives: San Clemente, California.
Height: 5–11. *Weight:* 180. Righthanded.
Career Highlights
Wimbledon: quarter-finalist 1969.
U.S. Pro: champion 1972.
Australian Open: semi-finalist 1971.
WCT Finals: quarter-finalist 1971, 1972, 1976.
Doubles (all with Stan Smith)
U.S. Open: champion 1968, 1974, 1978, 1980; finalist 1979.
Australian Open: champion 1970.
WCT World: champion 1973.
Wimbledon: finalist 1974, 1980, 1981.
French Open: finalist 1974.

One of the all-time great doubles players, Lutz and Stan Smith won four U.S. Opens and were three times runners up at Wimbledon. He and Smith are also the only pair to have won the U.S. national titles on all four surfaces: grass, clay, hard court and indoor. He returned after knee surgery in the early Seventies. Married to Sharon.

Ivanna Madruga-Osses

Born: January 27, 1961, Rio Tercero, Argentina.
Lives: Rio Tercero.
Height: 5–4½. *Weight:* 119. Righthanded.
Career Highlights
U.S. Open: quarter-finalist 1980.
French Open: quarter-finalist 1980.
U.S. Clay Courts: semi-finalist 1980.
Family Circle Cup: semi-finalist 1980.
Sunbird Cup T.O.C.: quarter-finalist 1980.
Murjani WTA Championships: quarter-finalist 1980, 1981.
Italian Open: semi-finalist 1980; quarter-finalist 1979, 1981.
Volvo Cup (Mahwah, New Jersey): quarter-finalist 1979.
River Plate (Buenos Aires): finalist 1977; semi-finalist 1978.
Argentine Open: champion 1979; finalist 1977.
U.S. Open Junior: finalist 1978.
Italian Open Junior: finalist 1978.
Federation Cup team: 1978–82.
Doubles
French Open: finalist 1980 (with Villagran).
Italian Open: finalist 1980 (with Villagran).

Ivanna Madruga was voted Most Impressive Newcomer in 1979 when

Ivanna Madruga-Osses.

she reached the Italian quarters and upset Sue Barker in the first round at Wimbledon. The Argentinian right-hander consolidated the success in 1980 when she reached the quarter-finals of the U.S. Open, the semis of the U.S. Clay Courts, the quarter-finals of the French and the Paris doubles final. She reached 16 on the singles computer in 1980. She was disappointing in 1981–82 but remains one of the best slow court players around. She has modelled her game on her hero, Guillermo Vilas.

Hana Mandlikova

Born: February 19, 1962, Prague, Czechoslovakia.
Lives: Prague.
Height: 5–8. *Weight:* 130. Righthanded.
Career Highlights
Wimbledon: finalist 1981.
U.S. Open: finalist 1980, 1982.
French Open: champion 1981; semi-finalist 1980, 1982.
Australian Open: champion 1980; quarter-finalist 1979.
Volvo Cup: (Mahwah, New Jersey): champion 1980, 1981.
Davison's Classic (Atlanta): champion 1980.
Italian Open: semi-finalist 1980.
New South Wales Open: champion 1979.
South Australian Open: champion 1979, 1980; semi-finalist 1978.
Toyota Classic (Melbourne): champion 1979; quarter-finalist 1978.
Murjani WTA Championships: finalist 1980.
Austrian Open: champion 1979; finalist 1980; semi-finalist 1978.
Federation Cup team: 1978–82.
Doubles
French Open: semi-finalist 1980 (with Tomanova).
Italian Open: champion 1980 (with Tomanova).

Hana Mandlikova.

A beautiful, elegant mover on court, as befits a girl whose father competed for Czechoslovakia in the 1956 and 1960 Olympic Games as a sprinter, 'Hanka' learned her tennis watching Martina Navratilova at the Sparta Club in Prague. She showed the benefit of the lessons by beating Martina on the way to the U.S. Open final in 1980. Her natural, free-flowing, attacking game leaves her vulnerable but is a joy to watch.

She fulfilled her potential by capturing the French title in 1981 and then reached the Wimbledon final where she froze against Chris Lloyd. A rather disappointing 1982 was highlighted by an appearance in the U.S. Open final – where she again lost easily to Mrs Lloyd.

Bruce Manson

Born: March 20, 1956, Los Angeles, California, U.S.A.
Lives: Fort Worth, Texas.
Height: 5–8. *Weight:* 150. Lefthanded.
Career Highlights
U.S. Open: quarter-finalist 1981.
Hong Kong: quarter-finalist 1981.
Houston: semi-finalist 1981.
Monterey: quarter-finalist 1981.
Denver: quarter-finalist 1981.
Doubles
Italian Open: finalist 1981 (with Smid).
La Quinta: champion 1981 (with Teacher).
Columbus: champion 1981 (with Teacher).
Cincinnati: champion 1980 (with Teacher).
Toronto: champion 1980 (with Teacher).

Bruce uses brain power to destroy the opposition. A shrewd tactician, the lefthander from Fort Worth, Texas, has now added consistency to his overall game. He's a fine doubles player and has had considerable success with Brian Teacher, winning both the Canadian Open and the ATP Championships in Cincinnati in 1980. Single.

Stacy Margolin

Born: April 5, 1959, Beverly Hills, California, U.S.A.
Lives: Beverly Hills.
Height: 5–3½. *Weight:* 112. Lefthanded.
Career Highlights
U.S. Open: last 16, 1978.
Women in Tennis Intl. (San Antonio): champion 1978.
Wells Fargo Open (San Diego): semi-finalist 1980.
Wimbledon Plate: quarter-finalist

1979.
USTA College Nationals: champion 1978.
U.S. Amateur Hard Courts: champion 1978.
U.S. National Under 21: champion 1977.

She is best known as John McEnroe's ex-girlfriend, which unfortunately obscures her own, rich talent. A psychology graduate at the University of Southern California, she unselfishly delayed turning pro until after she had helped her college to the national title in 1979. That cost her almost £10,000 as she had landed some fine results in that season's Avon Circuit. She is coached by her brother Mike, who also played for USC for four years. Stacy was U.S. Under 21 champion in 1977 and beat Tracy Austin while still at college. She has been a fine piano player since she was nine years old.

Regina Marsikova

Born: December 11, 1958, Prague, Czechoslovakia.
Lives: Prague.
Height: 5–9. *Weight:* 145.
Righthanded.
Career Highlights
Wimbledon: last 16, 1978.
U.S. Open: last 16, 1978, 1979.
French Open: semi-finalist 1977–78–79.
Italian Open: champion 1978; semi-finalist 1976, 1978.
Family Circle Cup: finalist 1980.
Canadian Open: champion 1977, 1978; quarter-finalist 1976.
Colgate Series Championships: fifth place 1979; eighth place 1978.
Avon Futures: champion 1980; finalist 1979.
German Open: champion 1981; finalist 1979; semi-finalist 1978.
Wimbledon Junior: finalist 1975; semi-finalist 1976.

Stacy Margolin.

Regina Marsikova.

Federation Cup team: 1978–82.
Doubles (with Teeguarden)
French Open: champion 1977.
Canadian Open: champion 1978.
U.S. Open: semi-finals 1980.

If she looks especially graceful on court it is because she was ranked No 3 figure skater in Czechoslovakia before she took up tennis full time. Another of the famous Prague 'school' like Mandlikova and Navratilova she had her best year in 1980, as a semi-finalist in the U.S. Open doubles and winning the Avon Futures. A fine painter, she has had her work exhibited in Prague.

Billy Martin

Born: December 25, 1956, Evanston, Illinois, U.S.A.
Lives: Palos Verdes, Estates, California.
Height: 5–10. *Weight:* 150. Righthanded.
Career Highlights
Wimbledon: quarter-finalist 1977.
Wimbledon Junior: champion 1973, 1974.
U.S. Open Junior: champion 1973, 1974.
Orange Bowl: champion 1973, 1974.
Auckland: semi-finalist 1981.
Doubles
Bristol: champion 1981 (with Simpson).
Newport: finalist 1981 (with Curren).

Although he is only 26, his best days already seemed to have passed him by. He completed a sweep of junior titles in 1973 and '74 when he won Wimbledon the U.S. Open and the Orange Bowl. In 1977 he reached the quarter-finals at Wimbledon, gaining a surprise win over Guillermo Vilas. His best ranking was 36 in 1974, but he plummeted into the 300's when he didn't play on the circuit in 1982. Married to Lotta.

Mario Martinez

Born: September 19, 1961. La Paz, Bolivia.
Lives: La Paz.
Height: 5–7. *Weight:* 145. Righthanded.
Career Highlights
U.S. Clay Courts: semi-finalist 1980.
Venice: champion 1981.
Nice: finalist 1981.
Washington Star: quarter-finalist 1981.

Mario comes from Bolivia's first family of tennis. His grandfather, Emilion, was the country's leading player throughout the Thirties and Forties, his father, Mario Snr. was No 1 in the Fifties and his uncle, Umberto Espanada, No 2. Together they formed the Davis Cup team. Mario and younger brother Marco are carrying on the tradition. Unknown outside South America, Mario announced his arrival by beating former Wimbledon champion Jan Kodes and Eddie Dibbs to reach the semi-finals of the U.S. Clay Courts at Indianapolis in 1980. Single.

Susan Mascarin

Born: June 28, 1964, Detroit, Michigan, U.S.A.
Lives: Grosse Pointe Shores, Michigan.
Height: 5–6. *Weight:* 110. Righthanded.
Career Highlights
U.S. Open Junior: champion 1980.
Italian Open Junior: champion 1980.
U.S. Amateur Clay Courts: semi-finalist 1979.
U.S. Girls' 16 Clay Courts: finalist 1980.
U.S. Girls' 16 Indoor: finalist 1978.
U.S. Girls' 14 Indoor: champion 1977.
Bonne Bell Cup team: champion 1978.

In 1980 she was one of the world's top juniors, winning the U.S. Open Junior, the Italian Open Junior and the Easter Bowl. With her record in U.S. Junior tennis she is a sure bet for the top. She reached the third round of the Italian Open in 1982.

Geoff Masters

Born: September 19, 1950, Brisbane, Australia.
Lives: Brisbane.
Height: 6–0. *Weight:* 155. Righthanded.
Career Highlights
WCT Finals: qualifier 1979.
U.S. Pro Indoor: quarter-finalist 1979.
Doubles
Wimbledon: champion 1977; finalist 1976 (with Case).
Australian Open: champion 1974 (Case); finalist 1976 (Case).

The player they call 'Bones' because of his slight frame always seems to produce his best form in doubles matches. He teams up a lot with fellow Australian Ross Case, with whom he won the Wimbledon title in 1977. Married to Anne-Marie with a son, Brett.

Andreas Maurer

Born: March 8, 1958. Gelsenk-Buer, West Germany.
Lives: Gelsenk-Buer.
Height: 5–7. *Weight:* 154. Righthanded.
Career Highlights
Berlin: semi-finalist 1978.
Stuttgart: semi-finalist 1981.

Brussels: quarter-finalist 1980.
Buenos Aires: semi-finalist 1981.

Well thought of on the circuit, Maurer is considered to be a rising star. His best wins have been over Balazs Taroczy and Jose Higueras. Single.

Alex 'Sandy' Mayer

Born: April 5, 1952, Flushing, New York, U.S.A.
Lives: Atherton, California.
Height: 5–10. *Weight:* 155. Righthanded.
Career Highlights
Wimbledon: semi-finalist 1973; quarter-finalist 1978; last 16 1979.
Doubles
Wimbledon: champion 1975 (with Gerulaitis).
French Open: champion 1979 (with brother Gene).
U.S. National Indoor: champion 1981 (with Gene).
U.S. Pro Championship: champion 1980 (with Gene).

The older of the two Mayer brothers, Sandy is a fierce critic of the on-court behaviour of many of his colleagues and wants to see the sport cleaned up. He hates the abuse McEnroe hurls at umpires and has been known to tell Nastase exactly what he thinks about his outbursts.

Mayer made his first big impression on the tennis world in 1973 when he became the NCAA singles and doubles champion and grabbed all the headlines at Wimbledon the same year by upsetting the favourite Ilie Nastase. Straight out of college, Sandy found himself in a Wimbledon semi-final, which he lost to Russia's Alex Metreveli. His prowess in tennis is not surprising, considering his background. He is the son of Alex Mayer, an international doubles representative for Hungary and Yugoslavia, who is now coaching in New Jersey. Sandy and his younger brother Gene are among the world's most formidable doubles combinations, and both are ranked in the top 12 of the doubles rankings.

Together, the brothers won the 1979 French Open doubles as well as the U.S. Pro Championship in 1980. Sandy has a Wimbledon doubles trophy as a result of his success with Gerulaitis.

Gene Mayer.

Gene Mayer

Born: April 11, 1956, New York, U.S.A.
Lives: Woodmere, New York.
Height: 6–0. *Weight:* 160. Righthanded.
Career Highlights
Wimbledon: quarter-finalist 1980, 1982.
U.S. Open: last 16 1981; quarter-finalist 1981.

French Open: last 32 1981.
WCT Finals: qualifier 1979.
Italian Open: semi-finalist 1979.
Doubles
French Open: champion 1978 (with Pfister), 1979 (with brother Sandy).
U.S. National Indoor: champion 1981 (with Sandy).
U.S. Pro Championship: champion 1980 (with Sandy).
U.S. Clay Courts: champion 1979 (with McEnroe).

The New Yorker who climbed to world No 4 in 1980 has succeeded despite a suspect temperament. His habit of pulling out of major tournaments with a variety of injuries has prevented him from claiming titles. He arrived in the big time mainly by winning the lesser-known tournaments. Gene plays with an over-sized racket and employs two-fisted shots both off the forehand and the backhand. A devout Christian, he also possesses a legendary appetite, being able to consume eight cheeseburgers at a sitting! Married to Rhonda.

Tim Mayotte

Born: August 3, 1960, Springfield, Massachusetts, U.S.A.
Lives: Springfield.
Height: 6–3. *Weight:* 180. Righthanded.
Career Highlights
Wimbledon: semi-finalist 1982; quarter-finalist 1981.
U.S. Open: last 32 1981.
Maui Grand Prix: finalist 1981.
NCAA: champion 1981.

One of the brightest young stars in tennis, Mayotte blazed into the Wimbledon semi-finals in 1982 to confirm his exciting potential. He is the latest sensation from John McEnroe's old *alma mater*, Stanford University. The youngest of eight children – five

Tim Mayotte.

brothers and two sisters – Tim has another brother, Chris on the pro tour. Remarkably consistent since stepping into the spotlight with a defeat of Connors in the second round of San Francisco in 1980.

He turned pro in June 1980 during the Bristol tournament. Articulate and easy going, he possesses a fierce competitive streak which seems certain to take him to the top. He is a strong server and volley player, suited to grass and fast about the court. Contrary to others of his generation he loves Wimbledon.

John McEnroe

Born: February 16, 1959, Wiesbaden, West Germany.
Lives: Douglaston, New York.
Height: 5–11. *Weight:* 160. Lefthanded.
Career Highlights
Wimbledon: champion 1981; finalist 1980, 1982; semi-finalist 1977.
U.S. Open: champion 1979, 1980, 1981; semi-finalist 1978, 1982.
Grand Prix Masters: champion 1979, 1981.
WCT Finals: champion 1979, 1981; finalist 1980.
French Open: quarter-finalist 1981.
Ornage Bowl: champion 1976.
Queens: champion 1979, 1980, 1981; finalist 1982.
Wembley: champion 1978, 1979, 1980, 1982; finalist 1981.
U.S. Indoors: champion 1980.
Australian Indoors: champion 1980, 1981.
French Junior: champion 1977.
U.S. Junior: eight titles.
Doubles (with Peter Fleming)
Wimbledon: champion 1979, 1981; finalist 1978, 1982.
U.S. Open: champion 1979, 1981.
Grand Prix Masters: champion: 1978, 1979, 1980.
WCT World Championships: champion 1979.
WCT Tournament of Champions: champion 1981.
Italian Indoor: champion 1978, 1979.
French Open mixed: champion 1977 (with Mary Carillo).

You either love him or hate him; no one can be complacent when John McEnroe is about. Sportswriters have reached for the vitriol to condemn his temperamental outbursts – Superbrat, Mac the Strife, the Incredible Sulk – but the public see him as more sinned against than sinner.

John himself says he is trying desperately to improve his behaviour and the pressures of it all seemed to have got to him in 1982, when he lost both the Wimbledon and U.S. titles and at one stage dropped as low as four on the world computer. McEnroe, a product of the redoubtable Stanford University, exploded onto the scene in 1977, when, as an amateur, he went all the way to the Wimbledon semis as a qualifier. He was the youngest ever semi-finalist and took a set off Jimmy Connors.

He decided against turning pro immediately and instead returned to Stanford for a year where he collected the national collegiate singles title, beating John Sadri in the final. He continued to make dramatic progress that winter into the world top five by taking the Grand Prix Masters title at Madison Square Garden in January 1979, defeating Ashe after being two match points down. He established himself as the second best player in the world behind Borg in 1979, by winning the WCT Finals in Dallas and the U.S. Open. In 1980 he lost an epic Wimbledon final to Borg but returned to beat the Swede the following year. His success, though, was marred by fierce squabbles with the All England Club. McEnroe's outbursts during his opening match brought a recommended fine of £5,000, then he ducked out of the traditional champions' dinner and the Wimbledon committee, for the first time, declined to make their new champion an honorary member. The bad taste left by it all was washed away in 1982 when Wimbledon

John McEnroe at Wimbledon 1982.

offered McEnroe membership after his five-set defeat by Jimmy Connors. It was scant compensation for McEnroe who, troubled by an ankle injury and the fatigue of five non-stop years, slumped sadly.

McEnroe was born on an American Air base in West Germany where his father was completing his national service. John Snr. is now a Wall Street lawyer and handles all his son's business and legal affairs. McEnroe's brother Patrick is also a tennis player. A keen rock fan, McEnroe relaxes with his guitar, which he plays well enough to occasionally make public appearances with good class bands.

Frew McMillan

Born: May 20, 1942, Springs, South Africa.
Lives: Transvaal, South Africa and London, England.
Height: 6–0. *Weight:* 155. Righthanded.
Career Highlights
U.S. Open: quarter-finalist 1972.
South African Open: finalist 1970.
Doubles
Wimbledon: champion 1967, 1972, 1978 (with Hewitt); semi-finalist 1979.
U.S. Open: champion 1977 (with Hewitt).
French Open: champion 1972 (with Hewitt).
WCT World: champion 1967 (with Hewitt).
Wimbledon Mixed: champion 1978, 1981 (with Stove).
U.S. Open Mixed: champion 1977, 1978 (with Stove).
French Open Mixed: champion 1966 (with van Zyl).
Davis Cup: champions 1974.

He is a consistent singles player who will always be remembered as one of the all time greats in doubles. The major doubles titles of Wimbledon, United States, France and the World Championship have all belonged to McMillan and his Australian-born, South African partner, Bob Hewitt.

McMillan has been a long-time Davis Cup representative for South Africa and helped his country to the final in 1974. Their final opponent, India, declined to play because of South Africa's apartheid policy. On similar grounds, McMillan and Hewitt were deported from Mexico prior to the start of the WCT World Doubles Championship in 1975. They were escorted under guard to the Mexico City airport and placed on a plane to the United States. As defending champions, they were granted a special challenge match the following week in Dallas which they lost to the Mexico City winners, Brian Gottfried and Raul Ramirez.

McMillan's trademarks are his white cap and the double-fisted shots he was playing before Borg made them fashionable. Married to Sally, with daughter Catherine and son Alex.

Peter McNamara

Born: May 7, 1955, Melbourne, Australia.
Lives: Florida, U.S.A.
Height: 6–1. *Weight:* 160. Righthanded.
Career Highlights
Australian Open: last 16 1975, 1978.
Berlin Open: champion 1979.
Swiss Open: finalist 1979.
Egyptian Open: finalist 1979.
Hamburg: champion 1981.
Doubles
Wimbledon: champion 1980, 1982 (with McNamee).

Peter McNamara.

WCT World Championships:
champion 1981 (with McNamee).

He is the best Australian player to emerge since the great era of Laver, Rosewall and Newcombe. The tall righthander became the first Aussie to reach the world top 10 since John Alexander in 1975, when he broke through in 1981. But he had first made his mark as a superb doubles player with his fellow Melbournian Paul McNamee. McNamara revitalised his singles game by switching to an oversized racket. His forehand improved immensely and he began a storming run at the start of 1981 which carried him to the German Open (beating Connors in the final), the Italian Open quarter final, the last 16 of the French and the quarters of Wimbledon where he fell to Borg. Late that year he became the first player to win a championship final under the penalty point system, when Gerulaitis was defaulted following disputed calls during an indoor tournament in Melbourne. Married to Kate with a son.

Paul McNamee

Born: November 12, 1954, Melbourne, Australia.
Lives: Sydney.
Height: 5–10. *Weight:* 160.
Righthanded.
Career Highlights
French Open: last 16, 1980.
Palm Harbour: champion 1980.
Bristol: semi-finalist 1981.
Stuttgart: quarter-finalist 1981.
Bastad: quarter-finalist 1981.
Doubles
Wimbledon: champion 1980, 1982 (with McNamara).
WCT World: champion 1981 (with McNamara).
Volvo Masters: finalist 1981 (with McNamara).
Australian Open: finalist 1980 (with McNamara).

Paul McNamee.

Paul McNamee went back to school just when he seemed likely to throw the towel in as far as tournament tennis was concerned – and he has never looked back since. The 'school' in question was Harry Hopman's tennis academy in Florida and after working on his game he left with a two-handed backhand and new hope for the future. That optimism was certainly well founded for, after Hopman's help in 1979, McNamee teamed up with fellow Aussie Peter McNamara and took the Grand Prix by storm. The following year the pair won the Wimbledon doubles title. Single.

Matt Mitchell

Born: March 16, 1957, Berkeley, California, U.S.A.
Lives: Los Altos, California.
Height: 5–11. *Weight:* 160. Righthanded.
Career Highlights
NCAA: champion 1977.
Doubles
Maui: champion 1981 (with Graham).

He stays consistently in the 100's on the computer. As an amateur he had glittering success. He was NCAA singles champion and an All American at Stanford University a year before John McEnroe in 1977. But as a pro he has never hit the headlines. Single.

Bernard Mitton

Born: November 9, 1954, Vryburg, South Africa.
Lives: Irvine, California, U.S.A.
Height: 6–1. *Weight:* 165. Righthanded.
Career Highlights
Newport: champion 1978; quarter-finalist 1980.
Costa Rica: champion 1979.
Johannesburg: finalist 1981.
Doubles
Johannesburg: champion 1981 (with Moore).
Tampa: champion 1981 (with Walts).
Richmond: champion 1981 (with Tim Gullikson).
Cologne: champion 1980 (with Pattison).
Stowe: champion 1980 (Pattison).
Davis Cup team: 1973–1978.

South African Mitton shouldn't even be playing tennis these days – but you just can't keep this determined player down. He had an operation for cataracts on his eyes in 1979, but made an astonishing recovery and now wears contact lenses. Despite having beaten Jimmy Connors and John McEnroe in his career, he's the first to admit that his game is a bit erratic. Married to Linda.

Terry Moor

Born: April 23, 1952, Hertford, Connecticut, U.S.A.
Lives: Memphis, Tennessee.
Height: 5–10. *Weight:* 160. Righthanded.
Career Highlights
French Open: last 16 1981.
Italian Open: quarter-finalist 1981.
U.S. National Indoor: quarter-finalist 1981.
Japan Open: champion 1979.
Doubles
French Open: finalist 1981 (with Teltscher).
ATP Tennis Games: finalist 1981 (with Teltscher).
WCT World: qualifier 1978 (with Cahill).

Terry didn't begin playing tennis until he had been at high school for a year.

But in the years since then he has stormed up the rankings list and reached the top 40 in 1979. That was the year he won the Japan Open and since then has usually been able to progress into the later rounds of most tournaments. Married to Judy.

Gilles Moretton

Born: February 10, 1958, Lyons, France.
Lives: Paris.
Height: 6–3. *Weight:* 180. Righthanded.
Career Highlights
French Open: last 16, 1979.
Linz: champion 1979.
Atlanta: finalist 1981.
Nice: quarter-finalist 1980.
Florence: semi-finalist 1981.
Doubles
Paris Indoor: champion 1979 (with Haillet).
Linz: champion 1979 (with Dominguez).

Moretton is reasonably successful although his exploits have been somewhat overshadowed by his countryman Yannick Noah. His best win was over José-Luis Clerc, whom he beat in the French Open to reach the last 16 in 1979. He once achieved the remarkable feat of beating two seeds in a day – Tomas Smid and Hans Gildermeister in Indianapolis in 1981. He has played in French Davis Cup team. Married to Christine.

Chris 'Buster' Mottram

Born: April 25, 1955, Wimbledon, Surrey, England.
Lives: Kingston, Surrey.
Height: 6–4. *Weight:* 175. Righthanded.
Career Highlights
Wimbledon: last 16, 1982; last 32 1977; junior finalist 1973.
U.S. Open: last 16 1980; last 32 1979.
French Open: last 16 1977; last 32 1979, 1980; junior champion 1973.
Davis Cup: finalist 1978; semi-finalist 1981.
British Under 21: champion 1971.

The British No 1 was undoubtedly born with the right genes. His father is Tony Mottram, former British Davis Cup player and national coach. His mother is Joy Gannon, who played Wightman Cup for Britain and was the centre of the early clothing 'colour ban' that preceded Gorgeous Gussy Moran. Buster's sister is Linda Mottram, a former professional on the women's circuit. And he was born at Wimbledon. Bap-

Buster Mottram.

tised 'Christopher' and nicknamed 'Buster', he is a graduate of King's College, London, where he studied Latin and ancient history. He was the youngest, at 16, to win the British Under 21 title. In 1972, when he was 17, he became the youngest Englishman chosen in Davis Cup. He won the French juniors in 1973 and was runner up to Borg at junior Wimbledon.

He was the toast of Britain when he led the team into the 1978 Davis Cup final for the first time since 1937. Mottram won eight of 10 matches, including a vital first-day defeat of Tony Roche in the semi-final against Australia and came from behind to beat Brian Gottfried in the final in Palm Springs. He slipped a little in the next two years but was back inside the world top 20 in 1982, when he reached the last 16 at Wimbledon.

Betsy Nagelsen.

Betsy Nagelsen

Born: October 23, 1956, St. Petersburg, Florida, U.S.A.
Lives: Venice, Florida.
Height: 5–9½. *Weight:* 135. Righthanded.

Career Highlights

Australian Open: finalist 1979.
Japan Open: champion 1979.
Virginia Slims of Newport, Rhode Island: finalist 1974.
Avon Futures Championship: champion 1977.
Wightman Cup team: 1974.

Doubles

Australian Open: champion 1979 (with Tomanova), champion 1980 (with Navratilova); finalist 1977 (with Reid).
Italian Open: finalist 1978 (with Mihai).
U.S. Open: semi-finals 1978 (with Shriver).

Betsy Nagelsen once had ambitions of swapping her racket for a set of drums in a rock group, but thankfully stuck with tennis and has been busy carving a solid career. She was a finalist in the 1979 Australian Open when she also won the doubles title. That remains her best big tournament but she won the Japan Open in the same year and the Surbiton Grass Courts title in 1981. The daughter of a dentist, she eventually plans a career in journalism.

Ilie Nastase

Born: July 19, 1946, Bucharest, Romania.
Lives: Ferrière, France.
Height: 6–0. *Weight:* 167. Righthanded.

Career Highlights

Wimbledon: finalist 1972, 1976.
U.S. Open: champion 1972.

French Open: champion 1973; finalist 1971.
Italian Open: champion 1970, 1973; finalist 1974.
WCT Finals: quarter-finalist 1974, 1977, 1978.
Grand Prix Masters: champion 1971, 1972, 1973, 1975.
WCT Challenge Cup: winner 1976, 1977, 1979.
Doubles
Wimbledon: champion 1973 (with Connors).
Wimbledon Mixed: champion 1970, 1972 (with Casals).
U.S. Open: champion 1975 (with Connors).
French Open: champion 1970 (with Tiriac).
Italian Open: champion 1970, 1972 (with Tiriac).

Ilie Nastase.

He is the enigmatic clown prince of the circuit. Arguably the most gifted player of the past decade, a creative artist with an inbuilt destruct mechanism that has become more apparent with the passing of the years. Nastase failed to win Wimbledon – losing to Smith in 1972 and Borg in 1976 – but by any other yardstick he must be judged as one of the greatest players. He won every other major title and was four times the Grand Prix Masters champion. In 1971 and '72 he led Romania to the Davis Cup final.

Despite the fading glory he is still a trump card for tournament directors who are assured of publicity wherever he appears. A natural ball player, Nastase could have made the grade as a footballer but chose the more glamorous world tennis circuit. Divorced from his Belgian model wife, Dominique, he has a daughter, Nathalie.

Martina Navratilova

Born: October 18, 1956, Prague, Czechoslovakia.
Lives: Dallas, Texas, U.S.A.
Height: 5–7½. *Weight:* 145. Lefthanded.
Career Highlights
Wimbledon: champion 1978, 1979, 1982; semi-finalist 1976, 1980.
U.S. Open: finalist 1981; semi-finalist 1975, 1977, 1978, 1979.
French Open: champion 1982; finalist 1975.
Australian Open: champion 1981; finalist 1974, 1982.
Italian Open: finalist 1974, 1975.
Colgate Series Championships: champion 1979; finalist 1978.
Avon Championships: champion 1979; finalist 1980.
Toyota Series: champion 1982.
Virginia Slims Championships:

champion 1978; finalist 1975.
German Open: finalist 1974.
U.S. Indoor: champion 1975.
Eastbourne: champion 1978, 1982; finalist 1979.
Federation Cup team: 1975 (Czechoslovakia); 1982 (USA).

Doubles

Wimbledon: champion 1976 (with Evert), 1979 (with King), 1981 with Shriver); finalist 1977 (with Stove.)
U.S. Open: champion 1977 (with Stove), 1978 (with King), 1980 (with King); finalist 1979 (with King).
French Open: champion 1975 (with Evert).
Italian Open: champion 1975 (with Evert).
Australian Open: champion 1980 (with Nagelsen).

One of the most powerful women players of all time, Martina proved virtually unbeatable in 1982 as she stormed towards a clean sweep of titles. With the Australian Open already in her locker from the previous year, she won the French Open and Wimbledon in impressive style. Under a lucrative arrangement with Playtex, she needed to add the U.S. Open to scoop one million dollars. But she was shocked by Pam Shriver in the quarter finals, losing in three sets and departing in tears.

Martina's father, Mirek, is an economist in Prague, and her mother, Jana, served as an official of the Czech Tennis Federation. She played Federation Cup for Czechoslovakia in 1975 and led them to the title before defecting to the United States to further her

Martina Navratilova after winning the BMW trophy at Eastbourne 1982.

career and collect her full share of the prize money. Her parents and sister were allowed to join her on an extended visit but found it impossible to settle and returned to Prague. Martina applied for U.S. citizenship in 1980 but this was not granted until almost two years later.

Martina at one time lived with feminist writer Rita May Brown and throughout the first half of 1982 was coached by sex-change woman Renee Richards. The partnership proved immensely successful as Martina won eight tournaments in a row. But the pair fell out at the end of Wimbledon and Renee returned to her practice as an eye surgeon.

Martina first took over the No 1 spot on the women's computer in 1978 after beating Chris Lloyd in the final at both Eastbourne and Wimbledon. She retained her Wimbledon crown the following year, again beating Mrs Lloyd in the final and was undisputed world No 1 on everyone's ranking list. Her domination seemed assured, yet she lost her way until 1982 when she entered that blinding run of form. Possessing a rather brittle temperament, she is nonetheless one of the most sporting players on the circuit and regarded with affection by most of her colleagues.

Yannick Noah

Born: May 16, 1960, Sedan, France.
Lives: Paris.
Height: 6–4. *Weight:* 175.
Righthanded.
Career Highlights
U.S. Open: last 16 1979, 1980, 1982.
French Open: quarter-finalist 1981, 1982; last 16 1980.
Italian Open: finalist 1980.
WCT Finals: qualifier 1981.

Yannick Noah.

The son of a First Division footballer in the French Cameroons, West Africa, Noah was discovered by America's great black champion Arthur Ashe during a tennis clinic in 1971. Ashe immediately contacted the French authorities and Noah was enlisted into their tennis school in Nice. He travelled with French teams from the age of 15 and quickly climbed to become French No 1. He created a controversy by admitting he used marijuana, a revelation he later denied.

An extrovert character, he enjoys fast motor bikes and loud music. His first major tour success came in 1981 – in Ashe's hometown of Richmond, Virginia. Noah, performing like a man possessed, crushed Gene Mayer, Roscoe Tanner and Ivan Lendl (who withdrew at 6–1 3–1) to take the title. '*It's my way of thanking Arthur for everything he has done*,' said Yannick. A natural, all-round athlete, Noah continued his rise last season by inflicting defeat on Borg at Monte Carlo. Single.

Beth Norton

Born: June 13, 1957, Bridgeport, Connecticut, U.S.A.
Lives: Fairfield, Connecticut.
Height: 5–3. *Weight:* 115. Righthanded.
Career Highlights
U.S. Open: last 16 1976.
Italian Open: quarter-finalist 1976.
South Australian Open: finalist 1978.
U.S. Girls' 18's: champion 1975.
U.S. Girls' 18 Hard Courts: champion 1975.
U.S. Girls' 18 Indoors: finalist 1974.
Orange Bowl International: semi-finalist 1975.
Doubles
U.S. Girls' 18 Indoor: finalist 1974.

As a junior in 1975 she was ranked first in the U.S. and No 5 in the world but has yet to justify that start. The following year she suggested big things were in store by reaching the last 16 of the U.S. Open and the quarters of the Italian Open. She is one of a family of 15. Her parents adopted two Vietnamese orphans, one from India and another from Hong Kong. A track star while at school, she enjoys horse riding.

Joachim Nystrom

Born: February 10, 1963, Skelleftea, Sweden.
Lives: Skelleftea.
Height: 6–0. *Weight:* 156. Righthanded.
Career Highlights
Bastad: semi-finalist 1981.
Geneva: semi-finalist 1981.
Madrid: quarter-finalist 1981.
Orange Bowl: champion 1980.

Orange Bowl winner in 1980 and is expected to be another Swede to watch for. In his first year on the circuit in 1981 he beat Victor Pecci, Jose Higueras and Australian Mark Edmondson. Single.

Gianni Ocleppo

Born: April 6, 1957, Turin, Italy.
Lives: Turin.
Height: 6–0. *Weight:* 175. Righthanded.
Career Highlights
Italian Open: quarter-finalist 1979.
Italian Indoor: finalist 1979.

When it comes to the fastest forehand around, Gianni Ocleppo must get a mention on anyone's list. His speed in that department is sizzling and, although he's not that fast on his feet, the shot really makes up for a great deal. The former Inter-Milan junior soccer player decided to make tennis his career after he had broken his leg during a football match. The move is now paying handsome dividends.

Manuel Orantes

Born: February 6, 1949, Granada, Spain.
Lives: Barcelona.
Height: 5–10. *Weight:* 165. Lefthanded.
Career Highlights
Wimbledon: semi-finalist 1972.
U.S. Open: champion 1975.
French Open: finalist 1974; semi-finalist 1972; last 16 1979.
Italian Open: champion 1972; finalist 1973, 1975.
German Open: champion 1972, 1975.
U.S. Pro: champion 1977, 1978.
U.S. Clay Courts: champion 1975, 1977.

Manuel Orantes.

Grand Prix Masters: champion 1976.
State Express Classic (Bournemouth): champion 1982.

Three operations on his golden left arm seemed to have finally taken their toll of the great Spaniard when seven months off in 1980 saw his ranking drop to below 150. But he returned in 1982 with all his old enthusiasm and charm to take the State Express Classic, the former British Hard Courts Championship, at Bournemouth. The son of a Barcelona lens grinder, Manuel joined the international circuit in 1966, when he became the first unseeded player to win the Junior Orange Bowl in Miami. Played his first Davis Cup match in 1967 and went on to capture the U.S. Open, Italian Open and Grand Prix Masters. Married to Virginia.

Marco Ostoja

Born: October 20, 1960, Bonn, West Germany.
Lives: Split, Yugoslavia.
Height: 5–9. *Weight:* 155. Righthanded.
Career Highlights
Mexico City: champion 1980.
Brussels: champion 1981.
Yugoslav Nationals: champion 1978.
Orange Bowl: semi-finalist 1977.
French Junior: quarter-finalist 1977.
Stowe: semi-finalist 1981.
Doubles
Kitzbuhel: finalist 1981 (with Sanders).

Ostoja was born in West Germany but plays for Yugoslavia in the Galea, Kings and Davis Cup teams. Ostensibly a clay court player, he won the Brussels tournament in 1981 without beating anyone of particular note. He was Yugoslav National Champion in the 14–16 and 18 age groups. But he has yet to move below 100 on the computer.

Leo Palin

Born: October 20, 1956, Helsinki, Finland.
Lives: Espoo, Finland.
Height: 5–5. *Weight:* 154. Righthanded.
Career Highlights
Top ranked junior in Finland: 1973, 1974.
Davis Cup team: 1980–1982.
Doubles
Lagos: finalist 1980 (with Johansson).

He makes a steady living without hitting the headlines, hovering around the 100 mark on the computer. He is Finland's No 1 player and leads their Davis Cup team. Single.

Adriano Panatta

Born: July 9, 1950, Rome, Italy.
Lives: Rome.
Height: 6–0. *Weight:* 180. Righthanded.
Career Highlights
Wimbledon: quarter-finalist 1979.
French Open: champion 1976; semi-finalist 1973, 1975.
Italian Open: champion 1976; finalist 1978; quarter-finalist 1979, 1981.
WCT Finals: quarter-finalist 1977.
Davis Cup: champions 1976; finalist 1977, 1979, 1980.

Panatta isn't just a hero back in his native Italy – he's an institution. Mention tennis over there and the talk will go straight to Panatta, whose exploits are already legendary, particularly on duty for his country in the Davis Cup, in which he has taken them into the finals in four out of the last six years. Panatta's best year was in 1976 when he stormed to the Italian and French titles in successive weeks. His flamboyant style of play makes him a clear crowd favourite wherever he plays. Married to Rosaria, with sons Niccolo and Allessandro and daughter Rubina.

Claudio Panatta

Born: February 2, 1960, Rome, Italy.
Lives: Rome.
Height: 5–10. *Weight:* 170. Righthanded.

Adriano Panatta.

Career Highlights
Italian Junior: champion 1978.
Doubles
Italian Nationals: champion 1980, 1981 (with brother Adriano).

The good-looking younger brother of heartthrob Adriano did extremely well in the South of France in 1982. He reached the semi-finals at Nice and at the same time was attempting to qualify for the Monte Carlo Open. He spent his time driving between the two sites. He is approaching the top 50 while Adriano is falling in the opposite direction. Married to Daniella with a son.

Onny Parun

Born: April 15, 1947, Wellington, New Zealand.
Lives: Wellington.
Height: 6–2. *Weight:* 170. Righthanded.
Career Highlights
Wimbledon: quarter-finalist 1971, 1972.
U.S. Open: quarter-finalist 1973.
French Open: quarter-finalist 1975.
Australian Open: finalist 1973.
Italian Open: quarter-finalist 1975.
Grand Prix Masters: qualifier 1974.
Doubles
French Open: champion 1974 (with Crealy).

The veteran New Zealander is still competing despite a number of neck operations in 1979 that would have ruined many a player. He can't move his neck too much while serving so he often attaches a string to his shirt collar which he bites on to ensure that his head and neck remain straight. A great competitor, whose best years were the mid-Seventies, he is married to Eva with two sons, Thomas and Phillip.

Andrew Pattison

Born: January 30, 1949, Pretoria, South Africa.
Lives: Scottsdale, Arizona, U.S.A.
Height: 6–2. *Weight:* 180. Righthanded.
Career Highlights
U.S. Open: quarter-finalist 1975.
Italian Open: quarter-finalist 1972.
Monte Carlo: champion 1974.
Johannesburg: champion 1974, 1979.
Palm Springs: quarter-finalist 1980.
Doubles
Newport: champion 1980 (with Walts).
Denver: champion 1981 (with Walts).
South Orange: champion 1981 (with Buehring).

Pattison was working on a Bachelor of Science degree in maths when he decided to give up and try for tennis. He's never looked back since and despite his age is still going strong. He lifted the Johannesburg title in 1979 and has made steady progress with his precision play. Married to Daphne with a son Sean.

Victor Pecci

Born: October 15, 1955, Asuncion, Paraquay.
Lives: Asuncion.
Height: 6–4. *Weight:* 185. Righthanded.
Career Highlights
French Open: finalist 1979.
WCT Forest Hills Invitational: semi-finalist 1979.
Doubles
Italian Open: champion 1978 (with Prajoux).
U.S. Pro Championship: winner 1978 (with Taroczy).
WCT World: finalist 1978 (with Higueras).

Victor Pecci

Victor Pecci is a national hero in his native Paraguay but he's the first to admit that it isn't quite the honour it seems at first. '*You see*,' he says, '*We only have about 200 tennis players back home*!' At 6ft 4in he is ideally built to frighten the living daylights out of lesser opposition – a task he accomplishes regularly. He did just that when he went unseeded right through to the final of the French Open in 1979, claiming the scalp of Jimmy Connors on the way. He teamed up with Belus Prajoux to win the Italian Open doubles in 1978. He wears a diamond ear-stud worth £1,000 and loves the pop group Dire Straits. Married to Mercedes.

Hank Pfister

Born: October 9, 1953, Bakersfield, California, U.S.A.
Lives: Los Gatos, California.
Height: 6–4. *Weight:* 185. Righthanded.
Career Highlights
Australian Open: semi-finalist 1981.
Doubles
Wimbledon: quarter-finalist 1980 (with Amaya).
U.S. Open: quarter-finalist 1981 (with Amaya); finalist, 1982.
French Open: champion 1978 (with G. Mayer), 1980 (with Amaya).
WCT World: finalist 1981 (with Amaya).
Australian Open: finalist 1981 (with Sadri).
Tokyo: champion 1980, 1981 (with Amaya).

Coached by his father since the age of five, the tall, powerful Hank has one of the biggest serve-volley games in the business, although it doesn't always fire as effectively as he would like. The death of his father during Wimbledon 1981 seemed certain to set him back. Instead he went out to win the singles tournament at Maui in Hawaii and dedicated the trophy to his parent. A severe ankle injury in 1977 and back trouble in later years have also proved troublesome. For a time he took to wearing a special corset to help correct his back problems.

An All American from San José State University, Pfister was unbeaten in college competition in 1975. A fine doubles player, he normally teams with the even taller Victor Amaya. Together they won the French Open in 1980 and reached the 1981 final of the WCT World Doubles Championships. Married to Kim with a daughter, Andrea Jane.

Hank Pfister.

Mary Lou Piatek

Born: August 6, 1961, Whiting, Indiana, U.S.A.
Lives: Munster, Indiana.
Height: 5–6. *Weight:* 128. Righthanded.
Career Highlights
U.S. Clay Courts: quarter-finalist 1980.
Wimbledon Junior: champion 1979.
U.S. Open Junior: finalist 1979; semi-finalist 1978.
Italian Open Junior: champion 1979.
French Open Junior: finalist 1979.
U.S. Girls' 18 Clay Courts: finalist 1979.
Canadian Open Junior: semi-finalist 1978.
U.S. Girls' 18 Hard Courts: champion 1979.

The world's top junior in 1979 when she won the junior titles at Wimbledon, and Rome and reached the U.S. and French finals. Her progress since then has been steady and she was a quarter-finalist in the U.S. Clay courts in 1980. She went out in the second round of both the French Open and Wimbledon in 1982.

Ulrich Pinner

Born: February 7, 1954, Zittan, West Germany.
Lives: Dortmund, West Germany.
Height: 5–9. *Weight:* 143. Righthanded.
Career Highlights
Swiss Open: champion 1979.
German Open: semi-finalist 1979; quarter-finalist 1976.

He was joint number one with Rolf Gehring in Germany and has an impressive Davis and Nations Cup record. He defeated Paul McNamee, Stan Smith and Paolo Bertolucci in the Nations Cup one year without losing a set. In the Davis Cup he beat José-Luis Clerc. He a soccer fan and lists music as a hobby. Married to Claudia, with daughters ters Elena and Eva-Marie and a son.

Pascal Portes

Born: May 28, 1959, Villeneuve, France.
Lives: Boulogne, France.

Height: 5–9. *Weight:* 153.
Righthanded.
Career Highlights
Paris Indoor: finalist 1981.
Bordeaux: semi-finalist 1981.
Florence: semi-finalist 1979.
Calcutta: finalist 1978.
Doubles
Italian Open: semi-finalist 1980 (with Noah).
Nice: champion 1981 (with Noah).

This young Frenchman proved conclusively that if you want to become known you have to collect a scalp or two on the tennis circuit. He did just that a couple of years ago by beating people like Jimmy Connors, Vijay Amritraj and Wojtek Fibak in the space of a few weeks. Now he's known as a solid performer the others must all regard warily.

Jerome Potier

Born: July 18, 1962, Rennes, France.
Lives: Paris.
Height: 6–1. *Weight:* 160.
Lefthanded.
Career Highlights
French Junior: champion 1979, 1980.
Bordeaux: finalist 1980.
Paris Indoor: quarter-finalist 1981.
Vienna: quarter-finalist 1981.

In 1982 he went up and down like a yo-yo. He came on the ranking list at 325 and played well enough to reach 116, but plummeted back into the 200's again. Single.

Barbara Potter

Born: October 22, 1961, Waterbury, Connecticut, U.S.A.
Lives: Waterbury.
Height: 5–9. *Weight:* 135.

Barbara Potter.

Lefthanded.
Career Highlights
Wimbledon: quarter-finalist 1982.
Eastbourne Under 21: champion 1978.
Women's Games (Salt Lake): semi-finalist 1980.
U.S. Open: semi-finalist, 1981.
U.S. Indoor: quarter-finalist 1978.
U.S. Girls' 18 Indoors: semi-finalist 1977, 1978.
Maureen Connolly Cup team: 1979.

This exciting serve-volley player delayed her entry to Princeton University to enjoy a taste of the international circuit and the signs are she will be an outstanding success. She has an interesting background: her grandfather won the Pullitzer Prize for international correspondents in 1943 and her father is a distinguished artist. Barbara has entered oil and water colours in State exhibitions. She beat Pam Shriver to reach the Wimbledon quarter-finals in 1982.

Belus Prajoux

Born: February 27, 1955, Santiago, Chile.
Lives: Santiago.
Height: 5–7. *Weight:* 155. Righthanded.
Career Highlights
Davis Cup: finalists 1976.
Doubles
Italian Open: champion 1978 (with Pecci).
Bordeaux: champion 1981 (with Gomez).
Vina del Mar: finalist 1981 (with Gomez).
Palermo: finalist 1981 (with J. Fillol).

Doubles are his forte, especially on clay. He gave Jimmy Connors a fright at the French Open in 1980, taking him to five sets before wilting under the pressure. He was a member of the Chilian Davis Cup team that ended 1976 as runners up to Italy. He also won the Italian doubles title with Victor Pecci in 1978. His ranking has stayed consistently in the 100's except for a spell in 1976 when he reached 66. He was ranked in the top 20 as a doubles player in 1982. Married to Hada.

Patrick Proisy

Born: September 10, 1949, Evreux, France.
Lives: Normandie, France.
Height: 5–11. *Weight:* 155. Righthanded.
Career Highlights
French Open: finalist 1972; quarter-final 1971.
Australian Open: semi-finalist 1973.
German Open: quarter-finalist 1974.
Hilversum: champion 1977.

His best years were the early Seventies when he reached the final of the French Open in 1972, losing to Andres Gimeno. He also reached the quarter-finals in Paris the previous year. He was runner up at the New Zealand Open in 1973 and reached the semis of the Australian Open in the same year. Married to Marion, with a daughter Daphne.

Mel Purcell

Born: July 18, 1959, Joplin, Missouri, U.S.A.
Lives: Murray, Kentucky.
Height: 5–10. *Weight:* 155. Righthanded.
Career Highlights
French Open: last 16 1981.
U.S. Clay Court: finalist 1980.
Tampa: champion 1981.
Atlanta: champion 1981.
Tel Aviv: champion 1981.
Doubles
NCAA: champion 1980

Mel Purcell.

Denver: finalist 1981 (with Stockton).

Son of a basketball and tennis coach, Mel took his first trip to Europe in 1977 at the age of 17. The experience on slow courts paid off for in 1980 he reached the final of the U.S. Clay Courts in Indianapolis. From No 555 in the world in 1978 he had risen to the edge of the top 20 three years later. Devastatingly fast on court and possessing all the enthusiasm of his hero, Jimmy Connors, Purcell looks booked for more success although his game is not yet geared for Wimbledon grass. ATP Rookie of the Year in 1980. Single.

Raul Ramirez

Born: June 10, 1953, Ensenada, Mexico.
Lives: Ensenada.
Height: 6–0. *Weight:* 165. Righthanded.
Career Highlights
Wimbledon: semi-finalist 1976; quarter-finalist 1975, 1978.
U.S. Open: quarter-finalist 1978.
French Open: semi-finalist 1976; quarter-finalist 1974, 1978.
Italian Open: champion 1975.
WCT Finals: quarter-finalist 1975, 1976, 1978.
Grand Prix Masters: qualifier 1974, 1975, 1976, 1977, 1978.
Doubles
Wimbledon: champion 1976 (with Gottfried); finalist 1979 (with Gottfried).
French Open: champion 1975, 1977 (with Gottfried).
Italian Open: champion 1974, 1975, 1976, 1977 (with Gottfried).
WCT World: champion 1975, 1980 (with Gottfried).

The handsome, moustacheod Mexican is one of the most elegant players on the circuit. Cutting down on his commitments these days to spend more time

Raul Ramirez.

with his business affairs. His father, Raul Snr., is the Under Secretary of State for Lower California in Ensenada, Mexico. He started playing at 12 under the guidance of former Mexican star Rafael Osuna. He studied business administration at the University of Southern California before joining the circuit. He was a member of the world's top ten from 1975 until 1980 and a brilliant doubles player, who won almost every tournament going with his good friend Brian Gottfried. Married to former Miss Universe Maritza Sayalero.

Pedro Rebolledo

Born: December 17, 1960, Santiago, Chile.
Lives: Santiago.
Height: 5–7. *Weight:* 152. Righthanded.
Career Highlights
Chilean Satellite Circuit: champion 1980.
Palermo: finalist 1981.
Venice: semi-finalist 1981.
Santiago: quarter-finalist 1980.
Barcelona: quarter-finalist 1981.
Madrid: quarter-finalist 1981.
Vina del Mar: quarter-finalist 1981.

A clay court specialist, he had a quiet time in 1982 by comparison with '81 when he was runner up in Palermo and made three quarter finals. His best wins are over Victor Pecci and Paul Ramirez. He has been a top 50 player since the end of 1980. Single.

Peter Rennert

Born: December 26, 1958, Great Neck, New York, U.S.A.
Lives: Los Angeles, California.
Height: 6–1. *Weight:* 160. Lefthanded.
Career Highlights
Australian Open: quarter-finalist 1979.
American Express/Lakeway: champion 1979.
Queens: quarter-finalist 1981.
Brussels: quarter-finalist 1981.
Doubles
Milan: finalist 1981 (with McEnroe).

Friend and doubles partner to John McEnroe, it may only be co-incidence that Peter has a degree in psychology. The bearded Californian met McEnroe at Stanford University, where he was runner up in the NCAA championship in 1980 to Robert Van't Hof and named College Player of the Year. He turned pro in 1979. Single.

Candy Reynolds

Born: March 24, 1955, Wichita, Kansas, U.S.A.
Lives: Knoxville, Tennessee.
Height: 5–8. *Weight:* 150. Righthanded.
Career Highlights
Wimbledon: last 16 1982.
U.S. Open: last 16 1980.
U.S. College Nationals: semi-finalist 1975.
Doubles (all with Paula Smith)
Wimbledon: semi-finals 1980.
U.S. Open: quarter-finals 1980.
French Open: quarter-finals 1980.

One of the world's top doubles players, she has been sought by a variety of partners. In 1980 she won the Volvo doubles with Navtratilova and the U.S. Indoors with Kiyomura. She has been a doubles semi-finalist at Wimbledon, Chichester, Eastbourne, Montreal, Richmond and San Diego plus quarter-finalist in the U.S. and French Opens – all with Paula Smith.

Kathy Rinaldi.

Kathy Rinaldi

Born: March 24, 1967, Jensen Beach, Florida, U.S.A.
Lives: Jensen Beach.
Height: 5–2. *Weight:* 130. Righthanded.
Career Highlights
Wimbledon: last 32 1982.
French Open: quarter-finalist 1981; last 16 1982.
German Open: finalist 1982.
U.S. 12s Group: champion Hard Courts, Clay Courts, Indoors and Nationals 1979.
U.S. 14s Group: champion Indoors 1980.

Kathy freely admits she has modelled her baseline game on her Florida neighbour, Chris Lloyd, and her intense concentration and unwavering nerve brought amazing success in 1981, when she beat Di Fromholtz and Anne Smith to reach the quarter finals of the French Open. Kathy's victory over the seeded Miss Fromholtz took place on Centre Court, but rather than displaying nerves, little Miss Rinaldi even had the temerity to ask for a line judge to be replaced – and had her request granted. Two weeks later the kindergarten killer became Wimbledon's youngest competitor for 74 years when, at the age of 14 years and 91 days, she made her appearance at headquarters thanks to a wild card entry. Kathy, daughter of a dentist, is the youngest of four children. When at home she jogs on the beach with her brown miniature poodle called Slugger. She became the first player to win all four U.S. Girls' 12s titles in the same year in 1979. In 1980 she played her first pro tournament. She had a year of consolidation in 1982 yet still managed to reach the French Open fourth round, beating Kathy Horvath on the way, before running into champion elect, Martina Navratilova, and losing in three sets. At Wimbledon she lost to Pam Shriver in the third round.

Christophe Roger-Vasselin

Born: July 8, 1957, London, England.
Lives: Boulogne, France.
Height: 6–2. *Weight:* 160. Righthanded.
Career Highlights
Munich: finalist 1981; quarter-finalist 1980.
Coupe Poree: finalist 1977.
Vienna: semi-finalist 1980.
Cincinnati: quarter-finalist 1980.
Doubles
Vienna: champion 1980 (Ocleppo).

As someone who began playing when he was eight, it's not surprising that

Christophe Roger-Vasselin is now one of the most solid performers around. He used the now banned 'spaghetti string' racket to reach the singles and doubles final at a Paris event a few years ago, but is now proving he can do it with no strings attached. Single.

Lucia Romanov

Born: April 28, 1959, Bucharest, Romania.
Lives: Bucharest.
Height: 5–5. *Weight:* 115. Righthanded.
Career Highlights
U.S. Open: last 16, 1980.
U.S. Open Junior: finalist 1976.
European Championships: semi-finalist 1979.
French Open: third round 1979.
French Open Junior: semi-finalist 1977.
German International Junior: champion 1977.

Lucia Romanov.

Romanian Nationals: champion 1979, 1980; finalist 1978.
Annie Soisbault Cup team: 1978–79.
Federation Cup team: 1978–82.

Lucia Romanov is one of the few qualified mechanical engineers on the women's circuit! She arrived on the U.S. scene with twin sister Maria in 1979. Maria, the Romanian champion, had beaten Lucia in the 1978 national final and was expected to do better, but Lucia adjusted well to the faster surfaces. She is elegant on and off court.

Joanne Russell

Born: October 30, 1954, Miami, Florida, U.S.A.
Lives: New York.
Height: 5–8. *Weight:* 135. Righthanded.
Career Highlights
Wimbledon: quarter-finalist 1982; last 16 1980.
U.S. Open: last 16 1980.
Family Circle Cup: semi-finalist 1978.
Player's Challenge (Montreal): semi-finalist 1980.
Davison's Tennis Classic (Atlanta): quarter-finalist 1980.
Wightman Cup team: 1977.
Doubles
Wimbledon: champion 1977 (with Cawley).

A great collector of sculpture and paintings, she is already insuring for the future by working part-time as a TV commentator. She had to recover from a serious tendon injury in her right foot in 1979 and dropped out of the world's top 100. But she recovered to battle her way to the Wimbledon quarter-finals in 1982. She has a delightful bubbly personality and is rarely lost for a good answer. She is a fine doubles player.

Virginia Ruzici

Born: January 31, 1955, Cimpia-Turzii, Romania.
Lives: Bucharest, Romania.
Height: 5–8. *Weight:* 128. Righthanded.
Career Highlights
Wimbledon: quarter-finalist 1978, 1981; last 16 1979, 1982.
U.S. Open: quarter-finalist 1976, 1978.
French Open: champion 1978; semi-finalist 1976; quarter-finalist 1979; finalist 1980.
Italian Open: finalist 1978, 1980. 1981.
German Open: finalist 1978; semi-finalist 1976, 1979.
Canadian Open: finalist 1978, 1980; semi-finalist 1976.
Colgate Series Championships: fourth place 1978.

Virginia Ruzici:

Swedish Open: champion 1980.
Austrian Open: champion 1980; finalist 1976.
Swiss Open: champion 1980.
Federation Cup team: 1973–76, 1978, 1980, 1982.
Doubles (all with Jausovec).
Wimbledon: finalist 1978; semi-finalist 1979.
U.S. Open: semi-finalist 1976.
French Open: champion 1978.
Italian Open: champion 1978; finalist 1976, 1981.
German Open: champion 1978.

Attractive, long-legged and dark haired, 'the Gipsy' comes from a sporting background – her father was a top Romanian professional footballer. She joined the circuit after graduating in PE from the University of Bucharest and proved just as dashing and lithe as Ilie Nastase. She moved steadily through the rankings before reaching No 8 in 1979. She has always threatened to win many titles but so far has collected only the French.

John Sadri

Born: September 19, 1956, Charlotte, North Carolina, U.S.A.
Lives: Charlotte.
Height: 6–2. *Weight:* 180. Righthanded.
Career Highlights
Wimbledon: last 32 1979.
U.S. Open: last 32 1978.
Australian Open: last 16 1978, finalist 1979.
Tokyo World Super Tennis: semi-finalist 1979.
Doubles
Wimbledon: semi-finalist 1979 (with Wilkison).
U.S. Open: quarter-finalist 1979 (with Wilkison).

John Sadri.

Kim Sands.

Nicknamed 'G.I. Joe' for his squat, solid build and fierce competitiveness, the individualistic Sadri is a fiery competitor, speedy around court and occasionally quick tempered. Ever a loner, he sported a skinhead haircut at college and still favours a short back and sides. A late developer, whose first taste of pro tennis was as a ball boy, he began to play the game seriously at North Carolina State University where he was coached for the first time. He modelled his mighty serve on John Newcombe and has improved his volley and ground strokes in recent years. Single.

Kim Sands

Born: October 11, 1956, Miami, Florida, U.S.A.
Lives: Miami.
Height: 5–7. *Weight:* 125. Righthanded.
Career Highlights
Eastbourne: third round 1980.
Citrus Bowl: finalist 1979.
Stuttgart: last 16 1980.
Rhode Island-WTA: semi-finalist 1978.
Doubles
Indiana WTA: finalist 1978.

The first black woman to win a scholarship to the University of Miami where she gained a degree in education and PE. One of the fittest, most dedicated professionals, she is coached by a former Olympic pole vaulter, Theodosios Balafas from Greece. She is a marvellous dancer and story-teller, who is rightly one of the most popular girls on the tour.

Nick Saviano

Born: June 5, 1956, Teaneck, New Jersey, U.S.A.
Lives: Plantation, Florida.
Height: 5–11. *Weight:* 165. Lefthanded.
Career Highlights
Wimbledon: last 16, 1980.
Cologne: finalist 1980.
Newport: semi-finalist 1980.

Linz: semi-finalist 1981.
South Orange: semi-finalist 1981.
Columbus: semi-finalist 1981.
Los Angeles: quarter-finalist 1981.
Stockholm: quarter-finalist 1981.
Doubles
Stuttgart: champion 1981 (with Mottram).

Give Saviano a mountainous task and then sit back and watch him fight like a tiger. The American may not have the elegance of some of his better known countrymen, but he certainly has an abundance of guts. Like in 1980 when he thrilled the Wimbledon crowd with his gritty battles against Eddie Edwards, Buster Mottram and Pat DuPré (all five-setters) to reach the last 16 unseeded. He's also beaten players of the calibre of Raul Ramirez, Stan Smith and Gene Mayer. Single.

Bill Scanlon

Born: November 13, 1956, Dallas, Texas, U.S.A.
Lives: Dallas.
Height: 5–11. *Weight:* 150. Righthanded.
Career Highlights
Wimbledon: quarter-finalist 1979.
New Zealand Open: champion 1981.
Australian Open: quarter-finalist 1981.
WCT Finals: quarter-finalist 1980.
WCT Invitational: champion 1981.
ATP Championships: quarter-finalist 1981.
NCAA: champion 1976.

A native of JR country in Dallas, 'Scaz' has found a second home in Hawaii where he regularly wins the local tournaments and plays guitar at beach parties. The Texan beat Fleming to win the national college title in 1976 while a student at Trinity University, San

Bill Scanlon.

Antonio. He collected the biggest pay cheque of his career in 1981, when he was an 11th hour invitee to the WCT event in Salisbury and beat Vijay Amritraj in five sets to pick up £50,000. Single.

Pam Shriver

Born: July 4, 1962, Baltimore, Maryland, U.S.A.
Lives: Lutherville, Maryland.
Height: 5–11. *Weight:* 130. Righthanded.
Career Highlights
Wimbledon: semi-finalist 1981; last 16 1980.
U.S. Open: finalist 1978; quarter-finalist 1980; semi-finalist 1982.
Australian Open: quarter-finalist 1980.
Sydney: champion 1980.
Canadian Open: semi-finalist 1980.
Player's Challenge (Montreal): semi-finalist 1980.

Pam Shriver.

Beckenham: finalist 1978.
Wightman Cup team: 1978, 1981.
Doubles
Wimbledon: champion 1981, 1982 (with Navratilova).
U.S. Open: finalist 1980 (with Stove); semi-finalist 1978 (with Nagelsen).
Chichester: champion 1979 (with Newberry); 1980 (with Du Pont).

This distant cousin to Sargent Shriver, the 1972 Democratic vice president nominee, is the original Yankee Doodle Dolly, born on Independence Day. The daughter of an insurance executive, she burst through in 1978 when she reached the final of the U.S. Open as a 16 year old. On the way she beat Navratilova in a semi-final containing two tie-breaks before losing to Mrs Lloyd.

The following year she experienced the first twinges of tendonitis which have plagued her ever since. After a special programme of exercise she and coach Don Candy came to Wimbledon in 1982 believing they could win the tournament. But Pam was surprisingly beaten by Barbara Potter in the fourth round. She proved she could live with the best, through, in the U.S. Open when she halted Navratilova's march on the Grand Slam with a three-set victory in the quarter-final.

Brigitte Simon

Born: November 1, 1956, Caen, France.
Lives: Caen.
Height: 5–4½. *Weight:* 122. Righthanded.
Career Highlights
French Open: semi-finalist 1978.
Ellesse Grand Prix Masters (Capri): champion 1979.
Nice: champion 1978; finalist 1977.
Monte Carlo: champion 1978, 1980; semi-finalist 1979.
Toulouse: finalist 1977.
Naples: champion 1978.
Federation Cup team: 1977–82.

She had to drop off the circuit for three months in 1977 because of a jaw bone operation, but returned to climb to the top 50. She became the first Frenchwoman since Francoise Durr to reach the last four of the French Open in 1978. She relaxes by playing guitar.

Hans Simonsson

Born: January 5, 1962, Fargary, Sweden.
Lives: Hylterbruk, Sweden.
Height: 5–11. *Weight:* 160. Righthanded.
Career Highlights
Wimbledon Junior: semi-finalist 1979.
European Under 18's: champion 1980.
European Under 16's: champion 1978.

Doubles
Linz: champion 1981 (with Jarryd).
Barcelona: champion 1981 (with Jarryd).
Bastad: finalist 1981 (with Jarryd).

This blond-haired Swede has never won a singles title in a pro-tournament but has steadily improved his world ranking after a year of travelling the circuit with a Swedish squad. He started life on the computer at 422 and has cut that to almost double figures now.

He is thought to be one of the stars of the future in the same mould as Wilander. He was European under-16 champion in 1978 and two years later he reached the semi-final of the Wimbledon junior event. He has had some success in doubles play partnering Anders Jarryd. He plays Davis Cup. He is the younger brother of Stefan.

Stefan Simonsson

Born: January 5, 1960, Hyltebruk, Sweden.
Lives: Hyltebruk.
Height: 5–9. *Weight:* 158. Righthanded.
Career Highlights
Swedish Junior Indoor: champion 1979.
Swedish Junior Outdoor: champion 1977, 1978.
Munich: semi-finalist 1980.
Galatina: finalist 1980.
Florence: quarter-finalist 1980.

Exactly two years older, to the day, than Hans. He reached the semi-finals of the Volvo event in Munich in 1980 – his best showing to date. He won the Swedish Junior indoor in 1976 and outdoor in '77 and '78. He started on the computer at 332, but now stands just outside the top 100. Single.

Russell Simpson.

Russell Simpson

Born: February 22, 1954, Auckland, New Zealand.
Height: 6–2. *Weight:* 175. Righthanded.
Career Highlights
New South Wales: semi-finalist 1980.
Linz: semi-finalist 1981.
Doubles
Bristol: champion 1981 (with Martin).
Monterrey: finalist 1981 (with Kriek).
Johannesburg: finalist 1981 (with Buehring).

Over the years this softly-spoken New Zealander has put himself about a bit since picking up a racket at the age of four. He has had career wins over Victor Pecci and Brian Gottfried and in 1982 took John McEnroe to 10–8 in the third set in a pre-Wimbledon tournament in Manchester. Now that Onny Parun has all but packed up playing, Russell is an important cog in the wheel that turns the New Zealand Davis Cup team. He helped them reach the semi-finals in 1982, the year he climbed to world No 67. He also won the doubles title with Billy Martin at Bristol in 1981. Single.

Pavel Slozil

Born: December 29, 1955, Opava, Czechoslovakia.
Lives: Prague, Czechoslovakia.
Height: 5–8. *Weight:* 155. Righthanded.
Career Highlights
French Junior: finalist 1973.
Nancy: champion 1981.
Munich: quarter-finalist 1980, 1981.
Florence: semi-finalist 1981.
Czechoslovakian Junior: champion 1973.
Czechoslovakian Nationals: champion 1973.
Doubles
Florence: champion 1981 (with Ramirez).
Boston: champion 1981 (with Ramirez).
Linz: finalist 1981 (with Drewett).
Nice: finalist 1981 (with C. Lewis).
Monte Carlo: finalist 1981 (with Smid).
Basle: finalist 1981 (with Gunthardt).

Pavel Slozil's emergence as a player to be reckoned with means Czechoslovakia now have a trio of powerful Davis Cup performers whenever he joins forces with Tom Smid and Ivan Lendl. He's an improving doubles player and is adding more and more power to the play that once made him his country's junior champion at singles, doubles and mixed doubles. Married to Jana.

Tomas Smid

Born: May 20, 1956, Pizen, Czechoslovakia.
Lives: Prague, Czechoslovakia.
Height: 6–3. *Weight:* 160. Righthanded.
Career Highlights
German Open: quarter-finalist 1979.
Spanish Open: quarter-finalist 1979.
South American Open: quarter-finalist 1979.
Davis Cup: champion 1980.
Doubles
Italian Open: champion 1979 (with Fleming).
German Open: champion 1979 (with Kodes).

The tall, cadaverous Czech had his finest hour on December 5, 1980 when he faced Adriano Panatta in the Davis Cup final in Prague. Smid ignored doctor's advice to play the Italian and fell two sets behind. But, despite stomach pains, he went on to win in five sets amid scenes of wild hysteria. The next day he and Lendl won the doubles to clinch the Cup. Smid, one of the crop of fine young players pouring out of Eastern Europe, was runner up in the junior Orange Bowl, Miami, when he was 18.

In 1976 the Czech Federation sent him abroad for further experience and he achieved his breakthrough by reaching the last 16 of the Italian Open on his way to the world's top 20. He has a fluid, all-court style reminiscent of Nastase. Married to Helena with son Tomas.

Tomas Smid

Anne Smith

Born: July 1, 1959, Dallas, Texas.
Lives: Dallas.
Height: 5–5. *Weight:* 117.
Righthanded.
Career Highlights
Wimbledon: quarter-finalist 1982.
U.S. Open: last 16, 1978, 1979.
Canadian Open: quarter-finalist 1980.
Central Fidelity Intl. (Richmond, Va): finalist 1980.
French Open Junior: champion 1977,
Orange Bowl: champion 1977; finalist 1976.
Doubles (all with Kathy Jordan).
Wimbledon: champion 1980; finalist 1981, 1982.
Wimbledon Mixed: champion 1982 (with Curren).
U.S. Open: semi-finals 1980.
U.S. Open Mixed: champion 1982 (with Curren).
French Open: champion 1980, 1982.
French Open Mixed: champion 1980 (with Martin).

Anne Smith.

Once the most valuable player of her high school basketball team although she is only 5ft 5in, she earned the nick-name 'Pepper' because of her liking for the Dr. Pepper soft drink. One of the world's best doubles players, she joined with Kathy Jordan to become the WTA's doubles team of the year in 1980. The devout Christian is also a fine singles player, as 21 U.S. nationals titles prove. She was the first American to win the French junior (in 1977). She reached Wimbledon quarter-finals in 1982.

Jonathon Smith

Born: January 29, 1955, Devon, England.
Lives: London.
Height: 6–2. *Weight:* 175.
Righthanded.
Career Highlights
Davis Cup: 1981, 1982.
Doubles
Auckland: finalist 1979 (with Jarrett).
Paris Indoor: finalist 1981 (with Jarrett).

The tall Devonian is at his best on grass but has proved inconsistent in singles. He forms a good doubles partnership with Andrew Jarrett and is a regular member of Britain's Davis Cup squad. He was educated at Millfield and the University of Oregon. He was an out-standing junior, winning all three British titles – covered, grass and hard court – in 1973. He ranked third in Britain in 1982. Married to Victoria.

Paula Smith

Born: January 10, 1957, Boulder, Colorado, U.S.A.
Lives: La Jolla, California.
Height: 5–7. *Weight:* 150.

Righthanded.
Career Highlights
Sunbird Cup T.O.C.: quarter-finalist 1980.
Greater Pittsburgh Women's Open: quarter-finalist 1979.
Indiana-WTA: semi-finalist 1978.
Missouri (USTA/Penn): champion 1979.
Perugia, Italy: finalist 1978.
U.S. Amateur Grass Courts: finalist 1976.
Doubles (all with Reynolds)
Wimbledon: semi-finals 1980.
U.S. Open: quarter-finals 1980.
French Open: semi-finals 1980, finalist 1981.

She hopes to become an ordained minister when she leaves the tour. She is one of the best women's doubles teams with partner Candy Renolds. Though born in Colorado, she was brought up on Maui in the Hawaiian Islands.

Stan Smith

Born: December 14, 1946, Pasadena, California, U.S.A.
Lives: Sea Pines, Hilton Head, South Carolina.
Height: 6–4. *Weight:* 185.
Righthanded.
Career Highlights
Wimbledon: champion 1972; finalist 1971; semi-finalist 1974.
U.S. Open: champion 1971, semi-finalist 1973.
Grand Prix Masters: champion 1970; finalist 1972.
WCT Finals: champion 1973; semi-finalist 1974.
Doubles
Wimbledon: finalist 1972 (with (Van Dillen), 1974, 1980 (with Lutz).
U.S. Open: champion 1968, 1974, 1978, 1980 (with Lutz), finalist 1971 (with Van Dillen).
French Open: finalist 1971 (with Gorman), 1974 (with Lutz).
Australian Open: champion 1970 (with Lutz).
WCT World: champion 1973 (with Lutz).

Stan Smith.

The first person to say Stan Smith is over the hill will be a brave one indeed, for the super-fit Californian has a habit of proving that he can go on and on. He'll be the first to admit that his best tennis days are now behind him but it won't stop him handing out reminders on court.

The former U.S. Army officer has a list of honours that would stretch down the Centre Court at Wimbledon, where he was champion in 1972, runner up in '71 and a semi-finalist in '74. He also won the U.S. Open in 1971. Along with Bob Lutz, he collected the U.S. Open doubles title four times.

He was a member of the American Davis Cup team for a decade for 1968 to 1978 and ended his stint with the best record in U.S. Davis Cup history. Married to Margie with two sons – Ramsey and Trevor.

Harold Solomon

Born: September 17, 1952, Washington, D.C., U.S.A.
Lives: Pompano Beach, Florida.
Height: 5–6. *Weight:* 135. Righthanded.
Career Highlights
U.S. Open: semi-finalist 1977.
French Open: finalist 1976; semi-finalist 1974, 1980.
German Open: champion 1980.
South African Open: champion 1975, 1976.
ATP: Champion 1980.
WCT Tournament of Champions: champion 1977.

A man of strong political beliefs, Solomon was caught up in the WCT – Volvo Grand Prix war as president of the Association of Tennis Professionals and his form suffered dramatically. From world No 7 he toppled out of the top 20 and did not win a tournament throughout 1980 or 1981.

A first class degree in political science at Rice University in Houston demonstrated where Harold's first love lay outside tennis, and he and his wife, Jan, are also deeply involved in the world freedom from hunger campaign. This 'thinking man's player' has been one of the greatest modern exponents on slow courts. 'Solly' reached the final of the French Open in 1976 where he lost to Panatta. In the semi-finals he drank 22 bottles of water while defeating Raul Ramirez in five sets on a blistering afternoon and still lost 13lbs.

Harold Solomon.

Sherwood Stewart

Born: June 6, 1946, Goose Creek, Texas, U.S.A.
Lives: Houston.
Height: 6–2. *Weight:* 185. Righthanded.
Career Highlights
Doubles
U.S. Open: finalist 1978 (with Reissen).
French Open: champion 1976 (with McNair), champion 1982 (with Taygan).
Grand Prix Master: champion 1976 (with McNair).
Italian Open: finalist 1977 (with McNair).
ATP: champion 1979 (with Reissen).

A late developer, Stewart is half of a formidable doubles partnership with Ferdi Taygan. A business degree with honours at Lamar University in Texas helped him to a top job with IBM computers. But on the advice of his friend, circuit pro Tom Gorman, he quit to try his hand at full-time tennis. His early doubles partner was Fred McNair, and then Marty Riessen. He and Taygan were late invites to the 1982 World Doubles Championships in Birmingham, where they reached the semi-finals. Stewart is also useful at singles as a 1977 victory over Borg proves. A keen skier, he owns a chalet in the Colorado

Rockies. Married to Linda with a daughter, Shastyn.

Dick Stockton

Born: February 18, 1951, New York City, U.S.A.
Lives: Dallas, Texas.
Height: 6–2. *Weight:* 180. Righthanded.
Career Highlights
Wimbledon: semi-finalist 1974.
U.S. Open: quarter-finalist 1976, 1977; last 16 1979.
French Open: semi-finalist 1978.
U.S. Pro Indoor: champion 1977.
WCT Finals: finalist 1977; semi-finalist 1976; quarter-finalist 1978.
Doubles
WCT World: champion 1977 (with V. Amritraj).
U.S. Open Mixed: champion 1975 (with Casals).
World Mixed: champion 1975, 1976, 1977 (with Casals).

Back trouble has plagued American Stockton in recent years and he has gone steadily down the rankings list since he appeared in the top ten back in 1978. He's battled on gamely despite the injury jinx that seems to stalk him these days. But, unless he makes a clear recovery, he'll be left with memories of his Wimbledon semi-final appearance in 1974 and his WCT doubles championship in 1977. Married to Sue with a daughter, Sarah.

Dick Stockton.

Betty Stove

Born: June 24, 1945. Rotterdam, Holland.
Lives: Alblasserdam, Holland.
Height: 5–11. *Weight:* 160. Righthanded.
Career Highlights
Wimbledon: finalist 1977; quarter-finalist 1975.
U.S. Open: semi-finalist 1977.
Colgate Series Championship: fifth place 1978, eighth place 1977.
Virginia Slims Champions: quarter-finalist 1972, 1977.
BMW Challenge: (Brighton): finalist 1978.
Porsche Classic (Stuttgart): finalist 1978.
Federation Cup team: 1966, 1969–72, 1976–80.
Doubles
Wimbledon: champion 1972 (with King); finalist 1973 (with Durr), 1975 (with Durr), 1976 (with King), 1977 (with Navratilova), 1979 (with Turnbull).
U.S. Open: champion 1972 (with Durr), 1977 (with Navratilova), 1979 (with Turnbull).
French Open: champion 1972 (with King), 1979 (with Turnbull).
Italian Open: champion 1979 (with Turnbull).
Wimbledon Mixed: champion 1978, 1981 (with McMillan).

U.S. Open Mixed: champion 1977, 1978 (with McMillan).

The powerful Dutch woman will always be known in Britain as Virginia Wade's opponent in the Centenary Wimbledon final. She has been president of the WTA three times and is on the ITF Committee of management. One of the world's great doubles players, she reached No 5 in the singles rankings in 1977. She speaks six languages and now coaches Hana Mandlikova.

Hana Strachonova

Born: January 2, 1961, Brno, Czechoslovakia.
Lives: Zurich, Switzerland.
Height: 5–5. *Weight:* 136. Righthanded.
Career Highlights
Wimbledon Plate: finalist 1978.
Argentine Open: finalist 1979.
U.S. Clay Courts: quarter-finalist 1980, 1981.

Hana Strachonova.

German Indoor: semi-finalist 1980.
Nice Open: semi-finalist 1980.
Turin: champion 1978.
U.S. Open Junior: semi-finalist 1976, 1977.
French Open Junior: finalist 1977; semi-finalist 1976.
Italian Open Junior: champion 1977.
Canadian Open Junior: champion 1977.
Orange Bowl: finalist 1977.
European Junior Championship: champion 1978.
Federation Cup team: 1978.
Doubles (with Paula Smith)
Swiss Open: champion 1979.
Argentine Open: finalist 1979.

In 1979, after her best ranking on the tour – 39, she defected from her native Czechoslovakia to live with an uncle in Zurich. She wanted to control her own career but has still to fulfill her promise.

Roscoe Tanner

Born: October 15, 1951, Chattanooga, Tennessee, U.S.A.
Lives: Kiawah Island, South Carolina.
Height: 6–0. *Weight:* 170. Lefthanded.
Career Highlights
Wimbledon: finalist 1979; semi-finalist 1975, 1976; quarter-finalist 1980.
U.S. Open: semi-finalist 1974, 1979; quarter-finalist 1972, 1980, 1981.
Australian Open: champion 1977.
WCT Finals: semi-finalist 1981; quarter-finalist 1975.
Grand Prix Masters: qualifier 1976, 1977, 1979, 1981.
WCT Challenge Cup: finalist 1978.
Davis Cup: champions 1981.

The 'Cannonball Kid' with a serve timed at 155 mph has blasted aside the best in his time. He beat Connors to

Roscoe Tanner.

reach the Wimbledon final of 1979 when he lost in five unforgettable sets to Borg. He took revenge in the U.S. Open a couple of months later to deny the Swede yet another chance of the Grand Slam. Unkindly referred to as a player with a serve looking for a game to go with it, Tanner has worked hard in recent years to improve his ground strokes and is now more of the complete competitor. He used to practise his serve for hours on end, aiming at Coke tins. Intelligent, son of a lawyer, Tanner has acquired an interest in a prosperous oil well and looks certain to concentrate on business matters within a couple of years. Married to Nancy.

Balazs Taroczy

Born: May 9, 1954, Budapest, Hungary.
Lives: Budapest.
Height: 6–0. *Weight:* 170. Righthanded.
Career Highlights
French Open: quarter-finalist 1976.
Spanish Open: champion 1978.
Dutch Open: champion 1978, 1979.
Belgian Open: champion 1979.
Doubles
WCT World: champion 1982 (with Gunthardt).

One of the gentlemen of the circuit, Taroczy is a superb touch player and a top flight doubles player with Heinz Gunthardt. In Europe, only Borg, Lendl, Fibak and Noah have been ranked above him in recent years. A linguist who speaks five languages fluently, the Hungarian properly introduced himself to British audiences by reaching the final of the British Hard Courts Championships in 1981, where he lost to Pecci in a match interrupted by snow. He returned to Britain and Birmingham in January last year to win the World Doubles with Gunthardt.

Ferdi Taygan

Born: December 5, 1956, Worcester, Massachusetts, U.S.A.
Lives: Framingham, Massachusetts.
Height: 5–8. *Weight:* 150. Righthanded.
Career Highlights
French Open: last 16 1980.
South African Open: semi-finalist 1979.
Doubles
ATP: champion 1981 (with McEnroe).
Canadian Open:champion 1981 (with Ramirez).
Wembley: champion 1981 (with

Stewart).
U.S. Open: semi-finalist 1981 (with Buehning).
Australian Indoor: finalist 1981 (with Stewart).
WCT World: semi-finalist 1982 (with Stewart).

Better known as half of the Stewart-Taygan doubles team, Ferdi was an outstanding junior player. He won the U.S. 18 year group championship, was four times an All American at UCLA and played Junior Davis Cup for the U.S. from 1972–75. Son of a civil engineer, Taygan is a curly-haired ball of fire on court. His favourite shot is the difficult backhand volley. Single.

Brian Teacher

Born: December 23, 1954, San Diego, California, U.S.A.
Lives: Los Angeles.
Height: 6–3. *Weight:* 175. Righthanded.
Career Highlights
Wimbledon: quarter-finalist 1982; last 16 1979.
U.S. Open: last 16 1980.
Australian Open: champion 1980.
Doubles
Canadian Open: champion 1980 (with Manson).
ATP Championship: champion 1980 (with Manson).

Strong serve and volley player who has made a steady rise since turning pro in 1976, moving into the top ten in 1981. He has proved injury prone and broke his ankle during the 1979 U.S. Open. A strained left ankle cost him valuable points in 1981, but he returned for a sucessful campaign. His lightning serve – he once hit 15 aces in a match against Tanner – carried him to the Australian Open title in 1980. The lanky Californian and Bruce Manson have also formed one of the most formidable doubles partnerships around. Married to former top woman player Kathy May.

Brian Teacher.

Pam Teeguarden

Born: April 17, 1951, Jacksonville, Florida, U.S.A.
Lives: Los Angeles,
Height: 5–10. *Weight:* 130. Righthanded.
Career Highlights
U.S. Open: quarter-finalist 1972.
Canadian Open: semi-finalist 1979.
Austrian Open: finalist 1975.
Avon Futures Championship: semi-finalist 1977.
Swiss Open: finalist 1972.
Swedish Open: semi-finalist 1975.
Chichester: finalist 1978.

Pam Teeguarden.

Doubles
French Open: champion 1977 (with Marsikova).
Canadian Open: champion 1978 (with Marsikova).
U.S. Open Mixed: champion 1974 (with Masters).

A former top junior, she comes from a tennis background. Her late father Jerry was one of the game's most respected teachers, working with many top players including Margaret Court and Virginia Wade and her brother Ron played for Michigan University. She dropped out of tennis for a year after leaving school to attend Berkeley and then UCLA. She wants to be a research scientist when she leaves the circuit.

Eliot Teltscher

Born: March 15, 1959, Palos Verdes Estates, California, U.S.A.
Lives: Palos Verdes.
Height: 5–10. *Weight:* 140. Righthanded.
Career Highlights
French Open: last 16 1979.
German Open: semi-finalist 1979.
Wimbledon Junior: finalist 1977.
U.S. Open Junior: finalist 1977.

Once rated by Nastase as '*the best young player in the world*' Teltscher has made steady if unspectacular progress to the world's top ten. His lack of recognition is partly explained by his strange refusal to play at Wimbledon which he regards as a hassle. An outstanding junior who reached the 1977 Wimbledon junior final and the U.S. Open junior final – beaten in both by Winitsky – and the Orange Bowl final – beaten by McEnroe – Teltscher was an All American in his first year at UCLA. He turned pro in 1977 and reached No 10 on the computer in October, 1980.

He was a finalist in the Italian Open last season where he lost to Andres Gomez. His volatile temperament has occasionally landed him in trouble, notably when he was fined for jostling an umpire during the French Open.

Andrea Temesvari

Born: April 26, 1966, Budapest, Hungary.
Lives: Budapest.
Height: 5–6. *Weight:* 136. Righthanded.
Career Highlights
Wimbledon: third round 1982.
French Open: third round 1982.
European Under 18: champion 1980.
Toyota Open, Lugano: finalist 1982.

Long-legged and with piercing blue eyes, Miss Temesvari seems destined to be a star both on and off the court. At the age of 15, she found herself serving for the match against that other teenage sensation, Andrea Jaeger, in the first round of the French Open. Her nerve wavered that time and she went on to lose in three sets to the No 2 seed, but it heralded the beginning of a run which took her from 144 in the world to inside the top 40 in 1982. Vera Sukova, the woman responsible for the explosion of talent in another Iron Curtain country, Czechoslovakia, says: '*For a child she is already a woman. For a beginner she can be a star. She has everything: a talent that is rare and an attitude that is refreshing.*'

Renata Tomanova

Born: December 9, 1954, Jindrichuv Hradec, Czechoslovakia.
Lives: Prague.
Height: 5–6. *Weight:* 130.
Righthanded.

Renata Tomanova.

Career Highlights
French Open: finalist 1976; quarter-finalist 1977.
Australian Open: finalist 1975; semi-finalist 1979.
Italian Open: finalist 1977; quarter-finalist 1973, 1980.
German Open: champion 1975; finalist 1976; quarter-finalist 1973, 1977, 1979.
Swedish Open: champion 1976.
Austrian Open: champion 1977, semi-finalist 1980.
Spanish Open: champion 1976.
Bonfiglio Cup (U–21): champion 1973–74.
World University Games: finalist 1977.
Federation Cup team: 1975, 1978–82.
Doubles (with Nagelsen)
French Open: semi-finalist 1980.
Australian Open: champion 1978.

Renata Tomanova is another of the Prague school and a striking blonde. She was coached by former Wimbledon finalist, Vera Sukova, and intends to work as a translator when she retires. She is at her best on clay but still reached the final of the Australian Open in 1975. Her lively personality makes her popular with players.

Thierry Tulasne

Born: July 12, 1963, Aiz-Les-Bains, France.
Lives: Paris.
Height: 5–10. *Weight:* 160.
Righthanded.
Career Highlights
U.S. Pro Indoor: semi-finalist 1981.
ATP Championship: quarter-finalist 1981.
Italian Open: last 16 1980.
Swedish Open: champion 1981.
Wimbledon Junior: champion 1980.
Italian Junior: champion 1980.

Thierry Tulasne.

Tulasne was an unknown 17-year-old Frenchman when he came up against Vitas Gerulaitis in the second round of the Italian Open. He hammered him 6–3, 6–3 to make people sit up and take notice. That was in 1980 and now the lad who also won the Wimbledon junior title that year has every reason to feel the rest of the Eighties hold nothing but good for him. Single.

Wendy Turnbull

Born: November 26, 1952, Brisbane, Australia.
Lives: Sandgate, Australia.
Height: 5–3. *Weight:* 120.
Righthanded.

Career Highlights
Wimbledon: quarter-finalist 1979, 1980, 1981, last 16 1978.
U.S. Open: finalist 1977; semi-finalist 1978.
French Open: finalist 1979.
Avon Championships: fifth place 1980; seventh place 1979.
Virginia Slims Championships: third place, 1978.
Colgate Series Championships: fourth place 1979; sixth place 1977; seventh place 1978.
Federation Cup team: 1977–82.
Doubles
Wimbledon: champion 1978 (with Reid); finalist 1979 (with Stove), 1980 (with Casals).
U.S. Open: champion 1979 (with Stove); finalist 1978 (with Reid).
French Open: champion 1979 (with Stove).
Italian Open: champion 1979 (with Stove).
U.S. Open Mixed: champion 1980 (with Reissen).
French Open Mixed: champion 1979 (with Hewitt), champion 1982 (with J. Lloyd).

They call her 'Rabbit' because of her ability to keep running all afternoon, but Wendy has been anything but a rabbit on the circuit, rising to the heights of world No 4 in 1979 and proving a worthy opponent for anyone on her day. She worked in a bank for four years in her native Brisbane after leaving school at 15. It was not until she was 24 that Wendy moved into the top level of the sport and it was another year before she reached a major final – the U.S. Open. That year, 1977, she jumped from 30th to 9th on the computer and was voted Most Improved Player. Australian Sports Personality of the Year in 1979, she had a doubles

Wendy Turnbull.

record that season with Betty Stove of 50 wins and just three losses as they collected the U.S. Open, French and Italian titles. She enjoys stamp collecting, music and swimming.

Gabriel Urpi

Born: August 16, 1961, Tarragona, Spain.
Lives: Tarragona.
Height: 5–8. *Weight:* 155. Righthanded.
Career Highlights
Orange Bowl: champion 1979.
Barcelona: quarter-finalist 1980.
Bordeaux: quarter-finalist 1981.
Sunshine Cup: champion 1979.

His ranking slipped into the 200's in 1982 after he seemed to be making steady progress. As a junior he had his biggest success to date winning the Orange Bowl in 1979. He is a member of Spain's Nations Cup team. Single.

Erik Van Dillen

Born: February 21, 1951, San Mateo, California, U.S.A.
Lives: Burlington, California.
Height: 6–0. *Weight:* 155. Righthanded.
Career Highlights
Newport: semi-finalist 1981.
Davis Cup: 1971–75.
Doubles
Wimbledon: finalist 1972 (with S. Smith).
U.S. Open: finalist 1971 (with S. Smith).
Australian Open: finalist 1977 (with

Pasarell).
Newport: champion 1981 (with Drewett).
Cleveland: champion 1981 (with Winitsky).

Erik was a member of the American Davis Cup team from 1971–75. An accomplished doubles player he reached the final of Wimbledon in 1972, the U.S. Open in 1971 and the Australian Open in 1977. He is the only player ever to win U.S. junior titles in singles and doubles in four age groups. Married to Lailee, with a son, Vincent.

Vince Van Patten

Born: October 17, 1957, Brooklyn, New York, U.S.A.
Lives: Sherman Oaks, California.
Height: 5–11.
Weight: 155.

Vince Van Patten.

Righthanded.
Career Highlights
Paris Indoor: semi-finalist 1979.
Lafayette: semi-finalist 1979.
Los Angeles: quarter-finalist 1979.
Maui, Hawaii: quarter-finalist 1979.
Tokyo: champion 1981.

Son of TV star Dick Van Patten, Vince started his acting career at the age of nine as the 'Bionic Boy' in the 'Six Million Dollar Man'. He began playing tennis and won a few small tournaments in 1977 which persuaded him to take up tennis full time. His decision was vindicated in sensational style as he beat Clerc, Gerulaitis and McEnroe to win the £150,000 World Super tennis event in Tokyo in November 1981. Former escort of Farrah Fawcett, his blond good looks seem destined for the pro circuit for many years.

Yvonne Vermaak

Born: December 18, 1956, Port Elizabeth, South Africa.
Lives: Glenconnor, South Africa.
Height: 5–1½. *Weight:* 116.
Righthanded.
Career Highlights
Wimbledon Plate: champion 1977; quarter-finalist 1979.
Murjani-WTA Championships: semi-finalist 1980.
South African Open: semi-finalist 1977, 1979; quarter-finalist 1978.
Family Circle Cup: quarter-finalist 1980.
World Tennis Classic (Montreal): semi-finalist 1978.
Canadian Open: quarter-finalist 1977–78.
Beckenham: champion 1977, semi-finalist 1978–79.
Avon Futures Championship: semi-finalist 1977.

Yvonne Vermaak comes from South Africa where her father, Audley, is a sheep farmer on a game reserve. Only 5ft 1½in tall, she is one of the smallest on the tour.

Guillermo Vilas

Born: August 17, 1952, Mar del Plata, Argentina.
Lives: Monte Carlo.
Height: 5–11. *Weight:* 165. Lefthanded.
Career Highlights
U.S. Open: champion 1977, semi-finalist 1975, 1976, 1982.
French Open: champion 1977, finalist 1975, 1978, 1982.
Australian Open: champion 1978, 1979, finalist 1977.
Grand Prix Masters: champion 1974.
Italian Open: champion 1980, finalist 1976, 1979.
WCT Finals: finalist 1976.

The handsome Argentinian, a part-time poet and confirmed romantic, is currently wooing Princess Caroline of Monaco after a year of celibacy. One of the great players of the Seventies the 'Young Bull of the Pampas' seemed to be losing his touch in 1981 but returned in 1982 with some impressive results. He has maintained a place in the top ten since 1974 when he captured the Masters on the grass at Melbourne.

His best year was 1977 when he won the French and U.S. Opens and strung together a 50-match winning streak. He lost his top ranking in Argentina to his great rival José-Luis Clerc in 1981, the year they combined to win the Davis Cup. He is coached by Ion Tiriac, the Romanian who guided Nastase's career. He boycotted Wimbledon in 1982 because of the Falklands Conflict. Single.

Guillermo Vilas.

Isabelle Villiger

Born: November 24, 1962, Zurich, Switzerland.
Lives: Herrliberg, Switzerland.
Height: 5–6½. *Weight:* 132. Righthanded.
Career Highlights
Wimbledon Junior: semi-finalist 1979, 1980.
U.S. Open Junior: quarter-finalist 1978.
French Open Junior: quarter-finalist 1980.
Monte-Carlo: finalist 1980.
Swiss Open: quarter-finalist 1978.
Nice Junior: semi-finalist 1979.
Monte Carlo Junior: semi-finalist 1979.
German Indoor: quarter-finalist 1980.
Federation Cup team: 1978–82.

Isabelle Villiger smashed her way into the Swiss top 10 in 1977 when she was a tender 15 years of age. Like most Swiss, she is multilingual and enjoys ski-ing. Coached by Andres Gimeno, she had a disappointing 1982, losing in the first round of the Italian and French Opens.

Mark Vines

Born: February 23, 1957, Richmond, Virginia, U.S.A.
Lives: Richmond.
Height: 5–7. *Weight:* 150. Lefthanded.
Career Highlights
U.S. Open: last 32 1981.
Paris Indoor: champion 1981.
Southwest Conference: champion 1976.

Vines made a dramatic leap on the computer in 1981 when he zoomed from 510 to 110. That year he won the Paris Indoor, defeating Harold Solomon and local favourite Yannick Noah on the way. He also reached the third round at the U.S. Open in 1981, but has since slipped back on the computer. Single.

Virginia Wade

Born: July 10, 1945, Bournemouth, Hampshire, England.
Lives: New York.
Height: 5–7. *Weight:* 128. Righthanded.
Career Highlights
Wimbledon: champion 1977; semi-finalist 1974, 1976, 1978.
U.S. Open: champion 1968; semi-finalist 1969, 1970, 1975.
Australian Open: champion 1972; quarter-finalist 1973.
French Open: quarter-finalist 1970, 1972.
Italian Open: champion 1971; semi-finalist 1970; quarter-finalist 1967, 1974, 1980.
Colgate Series Championships: third place 1977, 1978.
Virginia Slims Championships: semi-finalist 1974–75; fifth place 1977.
Virginia Slims Circuit: five titles 1971–77.
South African Open: finalist 1968, 1972.
Wightman Cup team: 1965–82.
Federation Cup team: 1967–82.
Doubles
Wimbledon: finalist 1970 (with Durr).
U.S. Open: champion 1973, 1975 (with Court); finalist 1972 (with Court); 1976 (with Morozova).
French Open: champion 1973 (with Court).
Australian Open: champion 1973 (with Court).
Italian Open: champion 1968 (with Court); 1973 (with Morozova).

She satisfied the British desire for romantic sporting heroines by winning Wimbledon in 1977, the tournament's Centenary year, when the final was watched by the Queen who was celebrating her Jubilee. Previously she had had a love-hate relationship with Wimbledon, usually failing to live up to the public's optimistic expectations. She won all the major championships except the French before virtually retir-

Virginia Wade.

ing in 1981, saying she would return to play Wimbledon 'just for fun'. Such was the nation's interest that even a change of hairstyle provoked columns of newsprint.

'Ginny' grew up in South Africa, where her father was Episcopal Archdeacon of Durban, but at the age of 15 the family returned to England and she went on to graduate from Sussex University in 1966 with a BSc in maths and physics. She was ranked No 1 in Britain for a record ten consecutive years and also holds the records for the most number of appearances in the Wightman and Federation Cup teams.

One of only five women to earn a million dollars from tournament competition, she published her autobiography *Courting Triumph* in 1978, the year after she was BBC TV Sports Personality of the Year. In 1982 she began a new career as a BBC commentator.

Sharon Walsh

Born: February 24, 1952, San Francisco, California, U.S.A.
Lives: Inclien Village, Nevada.
Height: 5–8. *Weight:* 140. Righthanded.
Career Highlights
Australian Open: finalist 1979.
Wimbledon Plate: finalist 1972, 1980.
South African Open: semi-finalist 1975, 1977.
Chichester: semi-finalist 1978; quarter-finalist 1980.
Wimbledon Junior: champion 1970.
Federation Cup team: 1971–74.
Doubles
Italian Open: finalist 1977 (with Bruning).
U.S. Clay Courts: champion 1973 (with Hogan).

Sharon Walsh has one of the most distinctive hobbies on the circuit – she collects fine wines. Tennis and competitive swimming vied for her attention in her teens, but she concentrated on tennis to become one of America's busiest players entering more than 25 tournaments a year. She played for the U.S. Federation Cup team in 1971–74. Best on grass, as she proved by humiliating Sue Barker in the first round of Wimbledon in 1982.

Trey Waltke

Born: March 16, 1955, St. Louis, Missouri, U.S.A.
Lives: Los Angeles, California.
Height: 5–8. *Weight:* 145. Righthanded.
Career Highlights
Vienna: finalist 1980.
Tulsa: finalist 1980.
Basle: semi-finalist 1981.
Maui: semi-finalist 1980.
Toronto: quarter-finalist 1980.
Cologne: quarter-finalist 1980.
Columbus: quarter-finalist 1980.
Doubles
Las Vegas: finalist 1981 (with De Latte).

Dreams can be shattered when you turn pro. Just ask Trey Waltke who made the move in 1974 but had to wait until 1980 before he could really say that he had arrived in the big time with final appearances in Vienna and Tulsa, plus the semis in Hawaii and the quarter-finals at Toronto, Columbus and Cologne. Single.

Kim Warwick

Born: April 8, 1952, Sydney, Australia.
Lives: Sydney.
Height: 6–0. *Weight:* 170. Righthanded.

Career Highlights
U.S. Open: quarter-finalist 1982.
Australian Open: finalist 1980; quarter-finalist 1981.
South African Open: champion 1980.
Italian Open: quarter-finalist 1977.
Doubles
Australian Open: champion 1978 (with Fibak), 1980 (with Edmondson); quarter-finalist 1981 (with Pfister).
Italian Open: champion 1980 (with Edmondson).
Davis Cup: semi-finals 1980, 1981.
Nations Cup: champions 1979.

Kim came under the wing of Vic Edwards, Evonne Cawley's legendary coach, at the age of 13. A strong serve and volley player in the best Australian tradition, he jumped 29 places on the computer in 1980 to finish at world No 22. But tendonitis in his shoulder, caused by a switch to a different weight racket, kept him off the tour for several months. He was bounced out of Wimbledon in the first round in 1982 in five sets by his countryman John Alexander, but reached the quarter-finals of the U.S. Open before running into Lendl.

He is rated by his fellow professionals as one of the gamest competitors around and overdue for his share of success. Married to Allana with a son, Kain.

Kim Warwick.

Anne White

Born: September 28, 1961, Charleston, West Virginia, U.S.A.
Lives: Charleston.
Height: 5–11. *Weight:* 140. Righthanded.
Career Highlights
U.S. Clay Courts: quarter-finalist 1980.
U.S. Amateur Clay Courts: champion 1980.
AIAW College National: quarter-finalist 1980.
U.S. Girls' 18s Indoors: finalist 1978.
U.S. Girls' 18s Hard Courts: finalist 1979.
Maureen Connolly Junior Invitational (Dallas): champion 1979.
Doubles
U.S. Girls' 18s Hard Courts: champion 1979 (with Piatek).
U.S. Girls' 18s: finalist 1979 (with Piatek).

She might have become a top flight basketball player had she not chosen tennis when she left St. Steven's High School for the University of Southern California – at 5ft 11in. she was tall enough.

Wendy White

Born: September 29, 1960, Atlanta, Georgia, U.S.A.
Lives: Atlanta.

Wendy White.

Height: 5–6. *Weight:* 125.
Righthanded.
Career Highlights
AIAW College National: champion 1980; finalist 1979.
National Collegiate Classic (Palm Springs): finalist 1980.
U.S. Amateur Hard Courts: champion 1979.
U.S. Amateur Clay Courts: finalist 1978.
U.S. Under 21 Clay Courts: finalist 1978.
Doubles
U.S. Open: quarter-finalist 1978 (with Kathy Jordan).

Wendy White managed to resist the lure of professionalism in 1980 when she came onto the circuit ranked 39 on the computer – the world's highest ranked amateur. The daughter of an Atlanta construction man, she decided to stay at Rollins College in Florida and continue her studies in business communication, although she wants to become a sports broadcaster or photographer. A fine doubles player, she teamed with Kathy Jordan to reach the U.S. Open quarter-finals.

Mats Wilander

Born: August 22, 1964, Vaxjo, Sweden.
Lives: Vaxjo.
Height: 5–10. *Weight:* 155.
Righthanded.
Career Highlights
Wimbledon: last 16 1982.
French Open: champion 1982.
Italian Open: semi-finalist 1982.
French Junior: champion 1981.
Bangkok: finalist 1981.
Stockholm: quarter-finalist 1981.

Everything happened for Wilander last season . . . and the signs are it is only the start of an outstanding career. Comparisons with Borg are hard to avoid, much as Mats hates them. He was only 17 when he claimed the French Open title – the same age as his millionaire countryman – he is blond, plays double-fisted shots and answers questions courteously and uncontroversially.

The unsung lad from Vaxjo might have created his sensation a fortnight earlier when he led Andres Gomez in the semi-final of the Italian Open but then lost his nerve. There was no such hiccup in Paris: Ivan Lendl, everyone's idea of the champion, was despatched in the fourth round, Gerulaitis followed in the quarters, Clerc in the semis and the new favourite, Vilas, in the final. At 17 years 288 days, Wilander was the youngest ever winner of a Grand Slam

Mats Wilander.

tournament. He was unprepared for the fuss, hiding away in his home when the world's Press came calling. *'I don't want any fuss,'* he said, *'I just want to be a tennis player.'*

Tim Wilkison

Born: November 21, 1959, Shelby, North Carolina, U.S.A.
Lives: Shelby.
Height: 5–11. *Weight:* 155. Lefthanded.
Career Highlights
Wimbledon: last 32, 1979.
N.S.W. Open: champion 1978.
New Zealand Open: champion 1979.
Doubles
Wimbledon: semi-finalist 1979 (with Sadri).
U.S. Open: quarter-finalist 1979 (with Sadri).

The word 'impossible' just doesn't figure in Tim Wilkison's vocabulary. That's why the impressive player from North Carolina always has a big following. He'll dive full length to connect with a shot if need be and the crowds love him for it. His all-go, swashbuckling style may not be liked by his opponents, but they can never accuse him of not trying. Single.

Van Winitsky

Born: March 2, 1959, Miami, Florida.
Lives: Lauderhill, Florida.
Height: 6–1. *Weight:* 165. Lefthanded.
Career Highlights
Hong Kong: champion 1981.
Japan Open: semi-finalist 1981.
Wimbledon Junior: champion 1977.
U.S. Open Junior: champion 1977.

The Wimbledon and U.S. Open Junior titles in 1977 convinced Winitsky that he should turn professional and since then he has made steady advancement up the world rankings list. A good doubles player, he gained a hat-trick of Grand Prix titles in his first full season as a pro. At 6ft 1in he has an extremely powerful serve and the only thing lacking in his impressive record so far are the singles successes that would make him even more of a man to watch. Single.

Ricardo Ycaza

Born: February 16, 1958 Guayaquil, Ecuador.
Lives: Guayaquil.
Height: 6–1. *Weight:* 160. Righthanded.
Career Highlights
French Open: last 16 1981.
U.S. Junior: champion 1976.

WCT Junior Invitation: champion 1977.
Brussels: finalist 1981.
Doubles
Santiago: champion 1980 (with Prajoux).
Sarasota: champion 1980 (with Gomez).
Quito: finalist 1981 (with Carter).

Five years ago Ycaza thought seriously about retiring, but was persuaded to give the game another try. The move turned out to be right and, as a member of the Bob Brett coaching stable, he's improving all the time. The former winner of the U.S. Open Junior and WCT Junior titles, is an accomplished doubles player. Married to Glenda.

Antonio Zugarelli

Born: January 17, 1950, Rome, Italy.
Lives: Rome.
Height: 5–10. *Weight:* 165. Righthanded.
Career Highlights
Italian Open: finalist 1977.
Bastad: champion 1976; semi-finalist 1977.
Davis Cup team: 1975–1980.
Doubles
Kitzbuhel: finalist 1979 (with Crealy).

Italian Zugarelli hit the highspots back in 1977 when he reached the finals of his own country's Open and met Vitas Gerulaitis. He lost, but did more than enough to prove he has the ability to survive the highest pressure. Married to Bruna with a daughter, Marcaela.

Acknowledgements

Data compiled by Tony Bodley, David Emery. Revised by Ron Mosey.

Photographs by All Sport/Tony Duffy and Bob Martin.